Palgrave Studies of Entrepreneurship and Social Challenges in Developing Economies

Series Editor
Rajagopal, EGADE Business School, Tecnológico de Monterrey, Mexico City, Mexico

This series explores the role of entrepreneurship in managing social challenges comprising poverty, gender inequality, sustainability and climate change, income disparity, social healthcare, community housing and homelessness, and clean food and water supplies across Asia, Africa, and Latin America.

Entrepreneurship in developing countries has an economic motivation and it is taken up as a survival occupation. The books in this series discuss various attributes of social enterprises, innovation, technology, and the role of leadership in meeting the recurring social challenges. The discussion on entrepreneurship in this book series is central to social entrepreneurship, family enterprises, entrepreneurial business models, disruptive innovation, consumer behavior, marketing-mix, branding, profit and performance, market expansion, new product development, operations and supply chain, manufacturing, and servitization. In addition, the volumes in this book series also address the PESTEL (political, economic, social, technological, environmental, and legal) perspectives that support socio-economic development.

Andrée Marie López-Fernández

Co-Creation in Social Enterprises

A Latin American Perspective on Human and Sustainable Development

palgrave
macmillan

Andrée Marie López-Fernández
Universidad Panamericana
Mexico City, Mexico

ISSN 2731-6874 ISSN 2731-6882 (electronic)
Palgrave Studies of Entrepreneurship and Social Challenges in Developing Economies
ISBN 978-3-031-83451-6 ISBN 978-3-031-83449-3 (eBook)
https://doi.org/10.1007/978-3-031-83449-3

Cover credit: Maram_shutterstock.com

This Palgrave Macmillan imprint is published by the registered company Springer Nature Switzerland AG
The registered company address is: Gewerbestrasse 11, 6330 Cham, Switzerland

Preface

What comes to mind first when you think about Latin America and the Caribbean? Do you think of the modern wonders Chichén-Itzá, Machu Picchu, the Incan Citadel, Christ the Redeemer, or ancient cultures such as the Aztecs, the Mapuches, and the Taínos and their contributions to civilization? Perhaps you first think of inventions and important contributions to science and technology, or the rich cuisines, languages, dances, sandy beaches, tropical rainforests, mountains, or glaciers? Does your mind fly to the soul-wrenching artistry of Frida Kahlo, the murals of Orozco, Rivera, and Siqueiros, or inspiring work of Botero, Munroe, and Lam? Perhaps the melodies of Lila Downs, Lolita Cuevas, Carlos Gardel, Chavela Vargas, Silvio Rodríguez, Violeta Parra, Gustavo Cerati, Compay Segundo, El Tri? Or the enchanted words of Neruda, Gray, Monterroso, Allende, Paz, Reidemann, Cortázar, Jara, Belli, or Mistral? And maybe, just maybe, your first thoughts are of revolution, despots, corruption, economic crisis, organized crime, poverty, impunity, natural disasters, power abuse, inequality, or guerillas.

The reality is that the region includes all the above and so much more; therefore, it is as complex as it is beautiful. Latin America and the Caribbean's diversity makes for a very interesting context for analysis; thus, much can be learned by studying this region's multidimensional and complex history as well as current dynamics. One of the aspects that has eluded the region is sustainable development; given the significant disparities observed in the region, social development is central to the discussion of the importance of social enterprises; in fact, it is central to all organizations. This led to the questions: What is the current state of sustainable development and human development in the region, particularly in relation to poverty, health, and housing? And, how have colonialism and dictatorships influenced current institution and organization dynamics as well as the need for social enterprises in Latin America and the Caribbean?

This book addresses the root causes for the region lagging behind in growth and development and discusses the importance of social enterprises and the roles of four groups of people in action who have the ability to co-create value for sustainable development. As the region is characterized by strong bonds that drive solidarity, how does collective behavior inform social enterprises' corporate philosophy and business dynamics? Stakeholders' growing concerns for the issues that permeate societies has meant an increase in their participation in social movements, both in person and online; thus, the different perspectives of stakeholders' actions in social enterprises to share responsibility, minimize social injustices, and maximize social growth and development are important elements for sustainable development.

A business model that is inclusive, socially responsible, and uses a profit-with-purpose approach, is not only strategic for social enterprises' performance, but also for micro and macro competitiveness, and current and future generations' well-being. Therefore, rethinking and redesigning the approach to business dynamics toward social and business growth and development makes good business sense for organizations across the board. It is my hope this book will contribute to existing literature and spark debates on the proposed concepts to further discussions that will bring us closer to sustained global business and social growth and development.

Mexico City, Mexico — Andrée Marie López-Fernández
November 2024

Acknowledgments I am grateful to Dr. Rajagopal for his mentorship and trust which have meant the world to me. This book would not have been possible without help and inspiration from family and friends; I am grateful for you all. I also express my gratitude to Renée Valentina López-Fernández and Ana J. Fernández Isla for their resolute encouragement. Dr. Sandra Elena Guevara Flores, thank you for sharing your expertise; and, Carla Patricia Sánchez Bernal, thank you for your unwavering support (YAMP).

Contents

List of Figures

List of Tables

CHAPTER 1

A History in the Making: Emerging Sustainable Development

Abstract Latin America and the Caribbean is a rich, diverse, and complex region. Certain historic salient events have driven the current *status quo* of social development in the region and, therefore, their analysis is of essence to understand the progress related to human and sustainable development. The reality is that the region is currently at an emerging sustainable development stage; as such, its advancement, or lack thereof, has been instrumental to the need for social enterprises.

Keywords People in action · Conquest · Colonialism · Dictatorships · Sustainable development · Human development · Emerging sustainable development

Practically all societal, economic, and political matters, as well as their corresponding processes and policies, are mirrored in Latin America (Kline et al., 2018). The current state of social issues that permeate societies in Latin America and the Caribbean are not a modern problem in the sense that they did not just occur because of poor current choices, or governance. Rather, the challenges the region is currently facing are derived from a history of structural violence, inequity, and inequality. This chapter begins with a description of what is considered to be people

A. M. López-Fernández, *Co-Creation in Social Enterprises*, Palgrave Studies of Entrepreneurship and Social Challenges in Developing Economies, https://doi.org/10.1007/978-3-031-83449-3_1

in action. The term Latin America and the Caribbean and the countries that the region encompasses is briefly reviewed; then, the history of Latin America and the Caribbean, as a region, particularly in relation to the effects of conquests, colonialism, and dictatorships on current progress, economic growth, and social development is discussed. An overview of the region's current standing in relation to sustainable development and human development is presented, followed by data related to its progress on poverty, social health, and housing, to understand the region's status on sustainable development and the association with the active participation of social enterprises.

People in Action

People act with various objectives in mind, either for primary interests (i.e., purpose, activity, task) or secondary interests (i.e., perceived benefit, financial gain). People in action are defined here as the individuals, organizations, as well as institutions, who, given their interests, have, are, and may participate in the need, creation, and potential success of social enterprises. There are four main groups of people in action; each group is explored and discussed throughout this book particularly in relation to their influence and impact on social enterprises and, in turn, poverty, social health, and housing in Latin America and the Caribbean. The first group, discussed in this chapter, includes those people who participated, in varying degrees, in shaping Latin America and the Caribbean's current state of affairs in relation to the progress, or lack thereof, of sustainable development. The second group, discussed in Chapter 2, consists of the architects of social enterprises; that is, the designers of the social missions that guide the enterprise's operations. The third group, examined in Chapter 3, encompasses the people that co-create value with and for social enterprises, and the fourth group, or the people who are recipients of the value created through social enterprises, are discussed in Chapter 4.

Latin American and the Caribbean

Although there is a debate regarding the origin of the term, it has been considered that Latin America was coined in the nineteenth century (Rojas Mix, 1986) by Francisco Bilbao (1823–1865), a Chilean politician, philosopher, and writer (Amiune, 2021), in 1856 in a conference in Paris (Arpini, 2014; San Martín, 2013); it was further disseminated by José

María Torres Caicedo (1830–1889), a Columbian diplomat, intellectual, and writer, in 1957 in the poem *Las dos Américas*, [the two Americas] (Marichal, 2015). In a postcolonial era, between the eighteenth and nineteenth centuries, integrationists' ideals and efforts led to the creation of integration systems and organizations in order to promote the economy and trade of countries across Latin America and the Caribbean (Herrera, 2017). According to the 2022 Revision of World Population Prospects, developed by the Population Division of the Department of Economic and Social Affairs of the United Nations Secretariat, Latin America and the Caribbean is considered one of the six geographical regions of the world (WPP, 2022). The diverse region encompassing North America, Central America, South America, as well as the Caribbean, according to the UN (2023a), includes thirty-three countries (see Table 1.1).[1]

Latin American and Caribbean countries have unique histories, cultures, and socio-economic conditions; therefore, the intention is not to group all countries in the region as one identity, rather to highlight their shared experiences. These, which are defined by unique attributes,

Table 1.1 Countries in the Latin American and Caribbean region

Antigua and Barbuda	Dominica	Nicaragua
Argentina	Dominican Republic	Panama
Bahamas, The	Ecuador	Paraguay
Barbados	El Salvador	Peru
Belize	Grenada	Saint Kitts and Nevis
Bolivia (Plurinational State of)	Guatemala	Saint Lucia
Brazil	Guyana	Saint Vincent and the Grenadines
Chile	Haiti	Suriname
Colombia	Honduras	Trinidad and Tobago
Costa Rica	Jamaica	Uruguay
Cuba	Mexico	Venezuela (Bolivarian Republic of)

Source Developed with data from: UN (2023a)

[1] The countries listed in Table 1.1 are those considered throughout this book when referring to the Latin American and Caribbean region as per the definition provided. Furthermore, the term Latin America and the Caribbean is used throughout the book, even when exploring a historic period when it had not yet been coined, in order to provide consistency.

geographic and migratory aspects encompassing the age of colonization to the present day (Castañeda, 2019), relate to colonial history, cultural diversity, political instability, economic, social, and environmental challenges, and a strategic geographical location, natural resources, potential growth, tourism, and developing infrastructure. These countries are considered to be emerging markets and countries in development; in 2017, these markets were responsible for approximately 80 percent of economic growth around the world (Gruss et al., 2017). According to Montiel (2011), emerging markets are those economies that have been financially associated with other more developed markets; therefore, they are able to stimulate economic growth internationally. They are countries that, despite their lower incomes, display significant growth or rapid growth (Emerging Money, 2012). While many may use emerging market and countries in development interchangeably, the difference may lay in the fact that the latter might have a somewhat slower economic growth and development, and the former a greater emphasis of economic growth over development.

It has always been a region that embraces a mosaic of peoples and cultures. Its biodiversity is vast (Ardisana & Gaínza, 2022); if we consider only South America, it accounts for "more than 40% of the Earth's biodiversity, more than one-quarter of its forests and is the single most biologically diverse area in the world" (Bovarnick & Alpizar, 2010, p. 2). For such reasons, amongst others, it is an attractive market for organizations around the world (Boisrobert et al., 2010) to invest and engage in commercial activities. Even though Latin America and the Caribbean is rich in natural resources, it has yet to reach its maximum capacity in relation to its productive potential (Nyssens et al., 2019); moreover, those natural resources are essential for the region's sustainable development (Bovarnick et al., 2010). However, there are several areas of opportunity including, but not limited to: the region's bioeconomy, effective institution and management of a circular economy, gender equality, sustainability (in terms of water usage and management, tourism, and energy), digital transformation for e-mobility and governance, manufacturing and geographical location of its production, food safety and security, and pharmaceutical and medical industries (Salazar-Xirinachs et al., 2023); all of which are important aspects for the region's growth and development.

Considering the potential, historical background, and existing challenges, it is important to examine Latin America and the Caribbean in order to grasp the possible impact of social enterprises and their influence on sustainable development. The first group of people in action in social enterprises first become apparent in the region's historical background. They forged the social, economic, and political fabric of the region; and, although the majority are no longer with us, the actions they took, some of which are discussed below, continue to influence the region's efforts toward sustainable development. Therefore, understanding such effects is important to explore their role in the advancement of social enterprises.

Latin America: A Historic Perspective

The countries in the region, while significantly diverse, share specific commonalities in terms of culture, language, struggles toward independence, as well as political, economic, social, and environmental crises. With a population of over 664 million people (CEPAL, 2023a), according to Prado (2021), it is a region that has been marked by poverty and inequality, lack of access to basic services, climate crisis, and social injustice, among others. In fact, according to the World Health Organization, in the last three years, "the number of people in need of humanitarian aid has nearly tripled" (WHO, 2023a, 2023b) in the region. Certainly, there are numerous reasons for these issues, some of which date back to the fifteenth and sixteenth centuries, such as the callous and brutal part of the region's history—conquest, colonialism, and, more recently, dictatorships—which have had profound humanitarian consequences.

The age of exploration of the Americas took place in the late 1400s, leading to the conquest and colonialism of Latin America and the Caribbean during the fifteenth and sixteenth centuries, led by Spain and Portugal. To be clear, Latin America had already been explored and inhabited by indigenous peoples' ancestors much earlier than when the Europeans "rediscovered" the region and called it the "New World" (Keller, 2016). There were various civilizations as well as empires across the region. According to Denevan (1992), there were approximately 53.9 million indigenous people when the region was "rediscovered" in 1492; however, by 1650, almost ninety percent of the population had been exterminated (Denevan, 1992). This fact alone makes abundantly clear that the region was not unoccupied; furthermore, the surviving marginalized groups were consequently subjected to a classist society based on a caste system (Vilaboy, 1997).

Imperialism and colonialism are different notions and events that may be viewed as occurrences at distinct points in history; however, the lines become blurred when acknowledging their intricacies, timeline, and consequences. While they have distinct characteristics, they also have many similarities; they both have had important and similar effects in relation to the political and economic control of the country in power (Kohn & Reddy, 2017), as well as social development implications. Imminent humanitarian crisis is one way of explaining each major change, or takeover, in the history of Latin America and the Caribbean.

Latin America was subjected to nearly three centuries of colonialism (Stern, 1985). Although most countries in the region were colonized by Spain, France, Portugal, the Netherlands, and Great Britain were also colonizers. European colonizers first reached the region between 1492 and 1620, then 1620 and 1720, and others arrived close to the twentieth century (Mark, 2020). While there were certainly a series of questionable and even barbaric actions, there are also arguments related to the positive effects that colonialism presented. For instance, Latin American and Caribbean countries' cultures are also influenced and shaped by other cultures such as African, Indigenous, and European, which has enriched the region, through art and cultural practices. While some may argue that language and cultural traits were a positive consequence of such actions, it is crucial to point out that the conquest cannot be remembered or analyzed without recalling the egregious transgressions because said enrichment was only possible by suppression, oppression, and annihilation.

The conquest, followed by the colonization, therefore caused serious harm. Álvarez (2016) has stated that "In the conquest all kinds of atrocities were committed and there was a systematic and premeditated policy of terror, necessary so a handful of conquerors could subjugate millions of natives throughout the American continent" (p. 166). In fact, it has been stated that there is a direct correlation amongst the current severe structural, political, social, cultural, and economic problems in the region with the colonial process (Barrantes, 1980). Further, Dussel (1967), has described Spain's unequal triumph as the "the supremacy of the ancient Mediterranean civilization over the pre-Hispanic American man. The entire pre-Hispanic civilization is defeated by the Spanish and taken advantage of as much as possible" (p. 44). Hence, it has had a direct influence on the underdeveloped status of many countries in the region. To such an extent that the slow pace at which countries in the region have progressed is directly associated with the consequences of endured subjugation.

While some nations were colonized once by one country, there were also countries that were colonized by multiple countries at different moments in time; in 1790, the independence movement initiated with Haiti's revolution (Vilaboy, 1997), however, some countries did not become independent until the early nineteenth century, including Cuba, the Dominican Republic, and Puerto Rico (Mahoney, 2003); therefore, their various battles for independence extended from 1804 (i.e., with Haiti's independence) to 1975 (i.e., with Suriname's independence). Table 1.2 includes the association of colonized countries, as they are known today in Latin America and the Caribbean, and the corresponding countries that colonized them.[2] Furthermore, there are currently countries in the region still identified as colonies by some authors, for instance, Puerto Rico (see Cruz-Martinez, 2019), which is an unincorporated territory of the United States, yet culturally Latin American. Moreover, it is noteworthy that various sources report different countries as colonizers of the same countries and territories.

According to Ypi (2016) "The evil of colonialism consists in the creation and defense of a political association that denies its members equitable and reciprocal terms of cooperation" (p. 140). While it might seem obvious, it is important to note that colonialism creates a clear distinction between the colonizers and the colonized, that is, the dominance of the former over the latter; further, in doing so, the colonized lack autonomy, voice, freedom, and are subjected to cultural imposition, cultural genocide, exploitation, and other social, political, and economic injustices. Consequences also included the massacre of indigenous groups, as well as the introduction of slavery. According to Fynn Bruey and Crawley (2024), it is estimated that approximately between 11.8 and 12.5 million African people were trafficked to the region and only about between 9.6 and 10.8 million arrived, which led to the subsequent normalization of slavery. It is noteworthy that such normalization is not only localized to the region, but is also observed internationally, across continents. In fact, even when slavery had been abolished, indentureship was implemented for over eighty years and approximately half a million South Asians were taken to the Caribbean as indentured workers

[2] The countries' names reflect their current designations rather than the names by which they were known prior to the corresponding conquest and colonization.

Table 1.2 Colonized countries in Latin America and the Caribbean

Country	*Colonizer(s)*	*Country*	*Colonizer(s)*	*Country*	*Colonizer(s)*
Antigua and Barbuda	Spain, France, Great Britain	Dominica	France, Great Britain	Nicaragua	Spain, Great Britain
Argentina	Spain	Dominican Republic	Spain	Panama	Spain
Bahamas, The	Spain, Great Britain	Ecuador	Spain	Paraguay	Spain
Barbados	Spain, Great Britain	El Salvador	Spain	Peru	Spain
Belize	Great Britain	Grenada	Spain, Great Britain, France	Saint Kitts and Nevis	Spain, Great Britain, France
Bolivia (Plurinational State of)	Spain	Guatemala	Spain	Saint Lucia	Spain, France, Great Britain
Brazil	Netherlands, Portugal	Guyana	Netherlands, Great Britain	Saint Vincent and the Grenadines	Great Britain, France
Chile	Spain	Haiti	France	Suriname	Netherlands
Colombia	Spain	Honduras	Spain	Trinidad and Tobago	Spain, Great Britain
Costa Rica	Spain	Jamaica	Spain, Great Britain	Uruguay	Spain
Cuba	Spain	México	Spain	Venezuela (Bolivarian Republic of)	Spain

Source Developed with data from (Britanica, 2023; CIA, 2023; Cruz-Martinez, 2019; De Santos, 2021; Department of State, 2009; ESA, 2023; Fernandez, 2022; Nohlen, 1993; Office of the Historian, 2023; Pozo, 2009; Quam & Campbell, 2023; Radbound University, 2023; The Permanent Mission of Saint Lucia, 2023)

(Singh, 2019), further strengthening the normalization of debt bondage and reinforcing the very foundation for modern-day slavery.

The reality is that colonialism has had varying effects on each country, leading to different problems and needs, and its legacies continue to influence the region. Colonialism brought historical and long-lasting consequences related to indigenous peoples' loss of sovereignty over their own territories (CEPAL, 2014). It has also resulted in the inherited internal *modus operandi* and discriminatory internal and external discourse; this, in turn, has also heightened several questionable attitudes and behaviors, for example, the misuse of terms such as third world countries, the obliviousness to all peoples which is clarified by the reference to all Latin Americans as Mexicans or Guatemalans, the inability to accurately identify Mexico as a part of North America as opposed to being part of Central America, as well as a string of stereotypes assigned to people from North to South America, which are not worth mentioning, amongst others.

Another consequence of colonialism, according to the Economic Commission for Latin America and the Caribbean (CEPAL), in terms of the countries' progress related to either their ability to sustain or grow, is that the region has encountered important limitations derived from "structural heterogeneity, external vulnerability, and the persistence of high levels of inequality" (CEPAL, 2014, p. 5). Therefore, there are significant implications regarding the countries' abilities to adopt transformational policies for scalability which require significant flexibility, adaptability, and operability. This further limits the possibilities of institutions and organizations to address past challenges as well as face new complications.

It has become apparent that colonialism has had a significant impact on political practice and dominance, commerce and market dynamics, as well as economic performance, with arguments for and against based on the consequences. That being said, there are far more arguments against colonialism and its very current aftermath, including but not limited to: civil violence, political rebellion, civil war (Lange & Dawson, 2009), systemic racism and intolerance (United Nations High Commissioner for Human Rights, 2022), geopolitical violence, structural violence, inequity, as well as prejudice both nationally and internationally, amongst many other aspects. In fact, the region has been subjected to a significant increase in conflict, violence, instability, and insecurity (WHO, 2024). This makes sense as colonialism is responsible for a series of patterns of questionable practices that have lasted long after the countries became independent (Barrantes, 1980).

The indigenous peoples' loss of autonomy, and sovereignty over their land also aided in the construction of countries that are "unequal, militaristic, and lacking future awareness" (Barrantes, 1980, p. 51). Decades after the last nation in Latin America was declared sovereign, and others self-governing, another form of oppression, yet not entirely distinct, overwhelmed the region. Almost half of the countries have historically endured and survived a type of dictatorship, including Argentina, Bolivia,

Brazil, Chile, Colombia, Cuba, Dominican Republic, Ecuador, Mexico, Nicaragua, Paraguay, Peru, Uruguay, and Venezuela (Arenas, 2005; Arratia, 2010; Rausch, 2016), either constitutional, military, and/or modernizing. Dictatorship has many definitions; however, it is commonly acknowledged as a system by which an individual or group take, or overtake, a government; the absolute power of a dictator provides authority to alter and/or violate the State's legislation (López et al., 2021) at the time of seizure of power or the *coup d'état*. Dictatorships, then, have further magnified colonialists' ideologies, and caused significant setbacks for organization and institution evolution, as well as the growth and development of each country.

Dictatorships are a direct cause of the loss of democratization. Amongst other aspects, this means that those upholding authority enact power without restriction, oversight, or any accountability whatsoever. During a dictatorship, freedoms and rights are suppressed and abused, which means a clear loss of individuals' sense of control. Further, in Latin America, it has often reflected a political system based on the process of the militarization of the State; the latter, in turn, brought forth authoritarianism; in consequence, a structure of violence that instigated "war against civil society and its traditional organizational structures [...] under the notion of an authoritarian State" (Victoriano Serrano, 2010, p. 181). Moreover, as a result, it is not uncommon to observe an *us-versus-them* rhetoric, as well as a clear distrust of authority (be it government, institutions, organizations, and/or big business). Statements are met with immediate disbelief and actions with skepticism; for instance, even when aid is provided by government institutions and/or businesses, there is a vexing and pervasive sensation that it is proffered with ulterior motives (whether political and/or profit driven), and if these did not exist, neither would the assistance. Although countries are able to transition to or back to a democratic system, it requires social, political, and economic reform which must be based on inclusion, diplomacy, and justice, at the very least. That being said, according to Kline et al., (2018), current characteristics in political and social tendencies in Latin America illustrate how the transition to a democratic region has not been accomplished. Therefore, proposing and following through on reforms that would foster social development is complex, to say the least.

The effects of colonialism as well as dictatorships have instituted a system of segregation and oppression, which has been long-lasting and still ignored in Latin America and the Caribbean to this day. One of its characteristics was an established hierarchical social system which, at present, is also embedded in organizational structures (mostly accredited as bureaucratic organizations), particularly in those whose mission is to serve a segment of or the entire population as a public function; in other words, those that had their origins in public policy. These include Secretariats, Institutions, Organisms, and Organizations focused on: health, housing, education, social development, national defense, public safety and security, justice and human rights, the environment, external relations, fiscal obligations, and tourism, amongst others. Despite intentions to democratically govern for all, far too many continue to be left behind—ignored. Evidence of this is the lack of access to basic services, in that, although everyone may be legally entitled to these services, policy execution upheld by a dividing discourse effectively marginalizes and ignores entire sectors of the population. Thus, this part of history has undoubtedly influenced the region's evolution and progress, or lack thereof. What is worse, current systems and practices show no sign of significant change which will most likely have a direct and negative impact on generations to come. The consistent use of force and questionable practices to indoctrinate societies into adopting hierarchical control systems and deem social justice, growth, and development as a luxury enjoyed by the lucky few, has also led to the current labor exploitation helmed by national and international organizations.

The process of decolonization brought forth the dismantling of control systems ingrained within current structures (Marañón-Pimentel et al., 2020). Decolonization suggests a resistance to the order prescribed since the conquest, however, not intended to be merely reduced to the notion that colonizers were bad and the colonized were good (Reyes, 2016). Supporters of postcolonialism in Latin America embraced the term to elucidate the region's political and cultural positioning in a globalized context, as well as to forge new connections with ideologies while condemning the lingering manifestations of colonialism (Pinedo, 2015). Recently independent countries aimed to forge their unique identities by strengthening their connections rooted in their history, culture, as well as politics (Herrera, 2017). Further, solidarity is engrained in the region's cultures and has been a driving force for their response to various social, political, and economic challenges. The cultures are widely known for their collectivism and hospitality, making their societies welcoming, warm, resilient, and cooperative. Solidarity economy, which can be traced back to pre-Columbian times (Gomes et al., 2012), engages communities who work together for financial and social benefits and is characterized by strong bonds rooted in their history, culture, and familiarity. It builds initiatives that serve purposes in healthcare, education, and environmental conservation (Gaiger, 2017), amongst others.

The postcolonial period, during the eighteenth and nineteenth centuries, also brought integrationist ideas with the aim of fostering economic and trade relations (Herrera, 2017). Such ideas led to the creation of a series of organizations to strengthen cooperation across the region, such as the Caribbean Community (CARICOM), Latin American Free Trade Association (ALALC), Central American Common Market (MCCA), Southern Common Market (MERCOSUR), Association of Caribbean States (AEC), Andean Community of Nations (CAN), Latin American Parliament (PARLATINO), and Bolivarian Alternative for Latin America and the Caribbean (ALBA) (Herrera, 2017), amongst others. Moreover, CEPAL was founded in 1948 and began operating as the Economic Commission for Latin America and the Caribbean in 1984 (CEPAL, 2023b).

As the region began to revert to democracy, in the 1980s, it faced several challenges related to the interconnected networks of society which had been impacted by vulnerable democratic systems and inequality (Peregalli & Ochoa, 2023). The process of democratization has been slow and often interrupted, as currently manifested in several countries in the region. The aftermaths of the above-mentioned historic events have left entire sections of the region's population in great and urgent need, which ought to be satisfied before considering a discussion on possibilities of growth and development. While there are many aspects that permeate society requiring urgent attention, there are three that should be of utmost highest priority: poverty, social health, and housing because they intersect with all dimensions of growth and development and are of the strongest determinants of disparities in the region.

Latin America and Sustainable Development

It is particularly interesting that there are multiple perspectives on the main issues that Latin America and the Caribbean currently faces; whereas some focus on social issues as the main problems, others find that economic growth is of greater importance. For example, Statista's research department developed a study with opinion leaders and journalists and reported that they consider the following, in order of perceived importance, as the problems that Latin America and the Caribbean are currently facing: job creation and economic growth, inflation and economic stability, insecurity, corruption, inequality, poverty, education, and health (Statista Research Department, 2023). Of course, economic growth is very important for the region's progress, however, poverty, extreme poverty, health, hunger, education, and housing are arguably more relevant in the sense that: (1) they exacerbate poverty and extreme poverty, and (2) economic growth is less probable to be sustained when these are not effectively addressed.

According to The World Health Organization (WHO), Latin America and the Caribbean is the "world's most economically unequal region and the second-most disaster-prone region" (WHO, 2023a). This is clear by the small number of families that hold the wealth of these countries, intensifying the bottom of the populations' pyramid, as well as the fact that three of every ten Latin Americans have faced a natural disaster since 2020 (UNDRR, 2023); just in 2023, the region faced dozens of forest fires in Chile, Argentina, and Honduras, droughts in Uruguay and Brazil, floods in Paraguay, Haiti, Argentina, and the Dominican Republic, floods, earthquakes, and landslides in Ecuador, and hurricanes in Mexico and Cuba, (IFRC, 2023; OPS, 2023a), amongst many others. These natural disasters put further strain on the respective governments' institutions, which are already heavily burdened, poorly funded or unfunded, and/or are operating under guidelines that strongly suggest avoiding the problem or merely putting a band-aid on it. Thus, the plight of a significant portion of the population is commonly minimized, to the extent that this reality has been normalized. Natural disasters, depending on their severity, also destroy ecosystems; any environmental degradation negatively impacts natural resources which are both used for society's basic needs as well as for the production of goods and services which ultimately serve other needs in society, and impact productivity at micro and macro levels. Thus, natural disasters also hinder growth and development.

Economic variables alone are insufficient to determine the overall development of a country. The Gross Domestic Product (GDP) has traditionally been used as a marker of a country's degree of progress; however, it is a measure of a country's productivity and growth (Kapoor & Debroy, 2019), but not a suitable indicator of human development. Kliksberg (2004) posited that one of the social problem fallacies in Latin America and the Caribbean is that growth alone is sufficient to determine development; the latter ought to be assessed by indicators that mirror the occurrences in fundamental aspects of people's everyday lives. Hence, it is essential to turn to alternative measures such as the Human Development Index and the Sustainable Development Goals to assess countries' development more comprehensively; both, which include economic variables but do not depend solely on them to determine the level of development, are used in this chapter to explore the development of countries in Latin America and the Caribbean. The Human Development Index was designed with the assertion that the primary criteria for evaluating a country's development should revolve around people as well as their capabilities, rather than exclusively focusing on economic growth (WHO, 2024). The Sustainable Development Goals were created to provide universal goals to achieve a standard of development globally.

According to the United Nations Development Programme (UNDP), Latin America and the Caribbean accounted for an average of 0.754 on the Human Development Index (HDI) in 2021 (UNDP, 2022), that is, a relatively high human development; however, about half of the countries in the region are in the bottom half of the ranking. Table 1.3 includes the Latin American and Caribbean countries analyzed along with their HDI rank and value for 2021. The HDI measures three dimensions (i.e., long and healthy life, knowledge, and a decent standard of living), four indicators (i.e., life expectancy at birth, expected years of schooling, mean years of schooling, and GNI (gross national income) per capita), as well as three dimension indexes (i.e., life expectancy index, education index, and GNI index) (UNDP, 2022). It is important to note that the results are reflective of the availability of data. It would seem that the region is not entirely devoid of human development; however, data may be at odds with the reality that countries in Latin America and the Caribbean are currently facing.

The urgent need to work toward development effectively and globally, led to the creation of the eight Millenium Development Goals (MDGs) in September 2000, to be met by 2015 (UN, 2015). Then, in 2015, the United Nations developed seventeen Sustainable Development Goals (SDGs) with the aim to "end poverty, protect the planet, and ensure that by 2030 all people enjoy peace and prosperity" (UNDP, 2023a); all seventeen goals are interdependent and synergistically have three main aims: "social, economic, and environmental sustainability" (UNDP, 2023a). The SDGs include "No poverty, zero hunger, good health and well-being, quality education, gender equality, clean water and sanitation, affordable and clean energy, decent work and economic growth, industry, innovation

Table 1.3 Human Development Index (HDI) in Latin America and the Caribbean

Country	*HDI value*	*HDI rank*	*Country*	*HDI value*	*HDI rank*
Chile	0.860	44	Brazil	0.760	89
Argentina	0.849	48	Colombia	0.758	91
Saint Kitts and Nevis	0.838	51	Guyana	0.742	95
Uruguay	0.830	52	Dominica	0.740	97
Antigua and Barbuda	0.826	54	Paraguay	0.731	102
Bahamas, The	0.820	57	Saint Lucia	0.725	108
Panama	0.820	57	Jamaica	0.706	115
Trinidad and Tobago	0.814	60	Belize	0.700	118
Barbados	0.809	62	Venezuela (Bolivarian Republic of)	0.699	119
Costa Rica	0.806	64	Bolivia (Plurinational State of)	0.698	120
Grenada	0.793	73	Suriname	0.690	124
Mexico	0.781	77	El Salvador	0.674	127
Saint Vincent and the Grenadines	0.772	81	Nicaragua	0.669	130
Dominican Republic	0.766	82	Guatemala	0.629	136
Ecuador	0.765	83	Honduras	0.624	138
Cuba	0.764	85	Haiti	0.552	158
Peru	0.762	87			

Source Developed with data from: UNDP (2022)

and infrastructure, reduced inequalities, sustainable cities and communities, responsible consumption and production, climate action, life below water, life on land, peace, justice and strong institutions, partnerships for the goals" (DESA, 2023).

These global goals set important indicators and standards for global sustainability that are imperative for Latin America and the Caribbean. The MDGs and SDGs are grounded in the definition of sustainable development, defined by the United Nations Brundtland Commission in 1987 and published in Our Common Future, which is also known as the Brundtland Report, as the "development that meets the needs of the present without compromising the ability of future generations to meet their own needs" (United Nations, 1987). The sustainable development goals have been developed to work toward the achievement of the 2030 Agenda for sustainable development, which has as its main principle to "Leave no one behind" (United Nations, 2023), with a particular effort to tend to the most vulnerable as well as those who have been consistently marginalized.

The effectivity of the SDGs directly depends on, in this case, countries' efforts to support the agenda. Latin America and the Caribbean countries' SDG scores are indicative of important efforts toward sustainable development. Table 1.4 includes Latin American and the Caribbean countries' SDG rank and scores, in other words, their percentage of achievement of the sustainable development goals. There are six countries, Antigua and Barbuda, Dominica, Grenada, Saint Kitts and Nevis, Saint Lucia, and Saint Vincent and the Grenadines, which have been indicated with an asterisk because they have not been ranked due to insufficient data.

It is important to note that the results are reflective of the availability of data. According to the United Nations Development Group (UNDG) of Latin America and the Caribbean, countries in the region "have been protagonists in the elaboration and adoption of the 2030 Agenda for Sustainable Development" (UNSDG, 2018); however, the reality is that despite the signs of inclusion of goals and indicators in government as well as organizational and business policies, there continue to be important disparities in the region.

Poverty, Social Health, and Housing in Latin America

There are a number of issues that are stalling progress toward sustainable development in Latin America and the Caribbean: poverty, social health, and housing are just three of them. These are of particular interest to the international community, the members of the United Nations and those that have pledged to strive toward the achievement of the seventeen sustainable development goals, amongst others; in fact, the United Nations sustainable development goals include specific goals and targets associated with all three elements. Further, they ought to be of the same importance and priority to not only State leaders, but also organizational

Table 1.4 Latin American and the Caribbean countries' SDG ranking and scores

Country	*SDG rank*	*SDG score*	*Country*	*SDG rank*	*SDG score*
Chile	30	78.2	Guyana	96	67.4
Uruguay	32	77.7	Panama	97	67.3
Cuba	46	74.1	Nicaragua	104	64.8
Brazil	50	73.7	Belize	107	64.6
Argentina	51	73.7	Trinidad and Tobago	114	63.0
Costa Rica	52	73.6	Honduras	116	62.9
Dominican Republic	62	72.1	Venezuela (Bolivarian Republic of)	117	62.9
Peru	65	71.7	Bahamas, The	124	60.9
El Salvador	73	70.7	Guatemala	127	59.4
Ecuador	74	70.4	Haiti	152	52.6
Colombia	76	70.1	Antigua and Barbuda	*	*
Mexico	80	69.7	Dominica	*	*
Jamaica	82	69.6	Grenada	*	*
Barbados	84	69.4	Saint Kitts and Nevis	*	*
Bolivia (Plurinational State of)	87	68.9	Saint Lucia	*	*
Paraguay	88	68.8	Saint Vincent and the Grenadines	*	*
Suriname	92	68.2			

Source Developed with data from Sachs et al., (2023)

leaders. The reality is that the basic needs of far too many people, particularly those residing in emerging markets and developing countries, are continuously ignored.

The first Sustainable Development Goal is "No Poverty", and it has seven targets and thirteen indicators (UN, 2023b); its aim is to eradicate extreme poverty, reduce the number of people living in poverty by at least fifty percent, and guarantee the equal rights of men and women in order to ensure "economic resources, basic services, ownership and control over land and other forms of property, inheritance, natural resources, appropriate new technology and financial services" by the year

2030 (UN, 2023b). The goal's indicators certainly present a difficult challenge; in fact, according to Adiel Guevara Rodríguez, "eradicating extreme poverty is the greatest and gravest global challenge" which must be "at the forefront of all international efforts" (UN General Assembly, 2023a). Table 1.5 includes the SDG rank and score, as well as the current progress of Goal 1 achievement and the countries' trends in its attainment. As can be seen, there are countries that, despite ranking in the SDGs, show unavailable data which means that there is a lack of reporting and disclosure. This is problematic because it entails a lack of transparency, perhaps even interest, as well as an impediment to understand the countries' progress; further, six countries are excluded due to the fact that there is insufficient data to rank in the SDGs (see Table 1.4). Only three countries have reported that they have achieved the goal; the results are somewhat aligned with other data on poverty in the region. Another three countries report that major challenges still persist, however, based on other data, it seems that the number could be higher.

It is unfortunately still noteworthy that women continue to have a high representation amongst the most vulnerable and poor, this is particularly true for black, Latin American, and Asian women. Despite the fact that some progress has been made, according to Azcona and Bhatt (2023), women do not have the same rights and opportunities as men in all countries around the world. In fact, there are over 380 million women and girls living in extreme poverty, which negatively impacts their access to education, health, adequate housing, decent work, voice, and power, amongst other basic needs (Azcona et al., 2022). The gender gap is one of the causes and is particularly concerning; in 2020, the World Economic Forum (WEF) stipulated that it would take over 150 years to close the gap globally and it would take Latin America and the Caribbean 59 years (Schwab, 2020). Moreover, the gender wage gap is at a 74.3% parity, and it will currently take approximately 53 years to close the gap (World Economic Forum, 2023). This means that although a slight improvement has been made within the last three years in the region, it is not nearly enough to eradicate poverty and reverse the effects by 2030. The wage gap, which is unacceptable and baseless, remains a strong determinant of not only poverty, but is also correlated with lack of access to healthcare as well as low quality healthcare, housing, and growth and development in general. Therefore, without profound change, it is not possible to break the poverty cycle in the region.

Table 1.5 Sustainable development goal 1—no poverty in Latin America and the Caribbean

Country	*SDG rank*	*SDG score*	*Goal 1. No poverty*	
			Dashboard	*Trend*
Chile	30	78.2	Significant challenges persist	Stagnating score or score is less than 50% increase of the required rate
Uruguay	32	77.7	Goal has been achieved	On course or score is maintained
Cuba	46	74.1	Unavailable data	Unavailable data
Brazil	50	73.7	Challenges persist	On course for goal achievement
Argentina	51	73.7	Challenges persist	Score is decreasing
Costa Rica	52	73.6	Significant challenges persist	Score is decreasing
Dominican Republic	62	72.1	Challenges persist	On course for goal achievement
Peru	65	71.7	Significant challenges persist	Moderate score improvement; score is insufficient for goal achievement
El Salvador	73	70.7	Challenges remain	On course for goal achievement
Ecuador	74	70.4	Significant challenges persist	Score is decreasing
Colombia	76	70.0	Significant challenges persist	Score is decreasing
Mexico	80	69.7	Significant challenges persist	Stagnating score or score is less than 50% increase of the required rate
Jamaica	82	69.6	Challenges persist	Stagnating score or score is less than 50% increase of the required rate
Barbados	84	69.3	Unavailable data	Unavailable data
Bolivia (Plurinational State of)	87	68.8	Challenges persist	Moderate score improvement; score is insufficient for goal achievement

(continued)

Table 1.5 (continued)

Country	*SDG rank*	*SDG score*	*Goal 1. No poverty*	
			Dashboard	*Trend*
Paraguay	88	68.8	Challenges persist	On course for goal achievement
Suriname	92	68.3	Unavailable data	Unavailable data
Guyana	96	67.4	Goal has been achieved	On course or score is maintained
Panama	97	67.3	Challenges persist	Moderate score improvement; score is insufficient for goal achievement
Nicaragua	104	64.8	Significant challenges persist	Stagnating score or score is less than 50% increase of the required rate
Belize	107	64.6	Major challenges persist	Score is decreasing
Trinidad and Tobago	114	63.0	Goal has been achieved	Stagnating score or score is less than 50% increase of the required rate
Honduras	116	63.0	Significant challenges persist	Stagnating score or score is less than 50% increase of the required rate
Venezuela (Bolivarian Republic of)	117	62.9	Major challenges persist	Score is decreasing
Bahamas, The	124	60.9	Unavailable data	Unavailable data
Guatemala	127	59.4	Significant challenges persist	Stagnating score or score is less than 50% increase of the required rate
Haiti	152	52.6	Major challenges persist	Stagnating score or score is less than 50% increase of the required rate

Source Developed with data from Sachs et al. (2023)

In addition to each country's conditions and policies, there are other factors that can disrupt progress; one of the most important disruptors in recent history was the COVID-19 pandemic. According to the World Bank, before the COVID-19 pandemic, however slow, extreme poverty was declining; yet, the pandemic increased the number of people in extreme poverty globally (The World Bank, 2022a). By March 2023, an estimated 659 million people were living in extreme poverty globally (Baah et al., 2023), and in September 2023, UNICEF and The World Bank reported that about one in six children lived in extreme poverty (UNICEF, 2023) around the world. And in less than four years, just between 2020 and 2023, 165 million people fell into poverty (UNDP, 2023b) around the world. Moreover, it has been estimated that approximately seven percent of the world will remain in extreme poverty in 2030 (The World Bank, 2022b).

According to the World Bank (2001), poverty is defined as the "pronounced deprivation in well-being". People who live in poverty are not only those who lack a dignified income but are also individuals who do not have access to the necessary resources to satisfy their basic needs (Alqassim & El-Setouhy, 2022). Despite its riches in natural resources, Latin America and the Caribbean are particularly disproportionate as the region accounts for the highest level of inequality (WHO, 2023a). The fact that the region is afflicted by poverty, people living with less than $2.15 a day, and extreme poverty, people living with less than $1.90 a day (The World Bank, 2022a), is not only alarming but also has a direct impact on other human development indicators including, but not limited to: nutrition, education, financial stability, equity, health, housing, equality, safety, and security, amongst others; therefore, poverty and extreme poverty are hindering growth and development. Poverty is more likely found in countries and regions that have endured systemic exploitation and oppression (Azcona & Bhatt, 2023), which is one of the reasons why it is so pervasive in Latin America and the Caribbean.

According to the Economic Commission for Latin America and the Caribbean (CEPAL), before the COVID-19 pandemic, in 2018, over thirty percent of the population in the region (i.e., Latin America and the Caribbean) was living in poverty and over 10 percent in extreme poverty (CEPAL, 2019). According to the WHO (2023a), there are approximately 86.4 million people currently living in impoverished conditions in Latin America and the Caribbean and given accelerated dynamics of inflation, there could be an estimated 1.1 percent increase of extreme poverty; the latter would also cause 7.8 million more people to be at risk in relation to food insecurity (WHO, 2023a), further escalating poverty. Food insecurity impacts and also derives from unequal and/or inaccessible, education, social capital, housing, and social health.

The third Sustainable Development Goal is "Good health and well-being" and has thirteen targets and twenty-eight indicators; it aims to "ensure healthy lives and promote well-being for all at all ages" (UN, 2023c). Some of its indicators include the reduction of maternal mortality, neonatal mortality, and deaths and illnesses from hazardous chemicals and contamination, halt newborn and children's preventable deaths, end epidemics, promote mental health and well-being, as well as "achieve universal health coverage, including financial risk protection, access to quality essential health-care services and access to safe, effective, quality and affordable essential medicines and vaccines for all" by 2030 (UN, 2023c). Table 1.6 includes the SDG rank and score, as well as the current progress of Goal 3 achievement and the countries' trends in its attainment. The data shows that none of the countries have achieved the goal; it also shows the countries as either stagnating or moderately moving in the right direction toward goal achievement. Further, six countries are excluded due to the fact that there is insufficient data for the SDG rank (see Table 1.4).

According to the World Health Organization's Constitution, which has been in force since 1948, health is considered to be a "state of complete physical, mental and social well-being", and a fundamental human right which is imperative in order to account for both peace and security (WHO, 2023b). According to the WHO's 2023 Health Emergency Appeal, as of January 2023, there are fifty-four health crises globally (WHO, 2023a) requiring urgent attention. These include not only disease outbreaks, but also natural disasters, climate-related health emergencies, and humanitarian crises which impact public health (WHO, 2023a); all of which create significant emergencies in emerging markets and developing countries.

There are many aspects contributing to poor social health in Latin America and the Caribbean; for instance, the frequent and intense emergencies and disasters that occur in the region significantly impact social health and, therefore, pose an important challenge to protect the health of their communities (WHO, 2023a). Further, people that live with HIV/Aids, about 2.5 million people (OPS, 2023b), the approximately 85 million living with a type of disability (Banco Mundial, 2021), as well as those with different sexual orientations and gender identities, are commonly marginalized in Latin America and the Caribbean, which ultimately creates important limitations and blocks them from gaining access to the healthcare system (UNSDG, 2018). And, in 2020, the total percentage of the gross domestic product (GDP) invested in health

Table 1.6 Sustainable development goal 3—good health and well-being—in Latin America and the Caribbean

Country	*SDG rank*	*SDG score*	*Goal 3. Good health and well-being*	
			Dashboard	*Trend*
Chile	30	78.2	Challenges persist	Moderate score improvement; score is insufficient for goal achievement
Uruguay	32	77.7	Significant challenges persist	Moderate score improvement; score is insufficient for goal achievement
Cuba	46	74.1	Significant challenges persist	Stagnating score or score is less than 50% increase of the required rate
Brazil	50	73.7	Significant challenges persist	Moderate score improvement; score is insufficient for goal achievement
Argentina	51	73.7	Significant challenges persist	Stagnating score or score is less than 50% increase of the required rate
Costa Rica	52	73.6	Significant challenges persist	Moderate score improvement; score is insufficient for goal achievement
Dominican Republic	62	72.1	Major challenges persist	Stagnating score or score is less than 50% increase of the required rate
Peru	65	71.7	Major challenges persist	Moderate score improvement; score is insufficient for goal achievement
El Salvador	73	70.7	Major challenges persist	Moderate score improvement; score is insufficient for goal achievement
Ecuador	74	70.4	Major challenges persist	Moderate score improvement; score is insufficient for goal achievement
Colombia	76	70.0	Major challenges persist	Moderate score improvement; score is insufficient for goal achievement
Mexico	80	69.7	Major challenges persist	Moderate score improvement; score is insufficient for goal achievement
Jamaica	82	69.6	Significant challenges persist	Stagnating score or score is less than 50% increase of the required rate

(continued)

Table 1.6 (continued)

Country	*SDG rank*	*SDG score*	*Goal 3. Good health and well-being*	
			Dashboard	*Trend*
Barbados	84	69.3	Significant challenges persist	Moderate score improvement; score is insufficient for goal achievement
Bolivia (Plurinational State of)	87	68.8	Major challenges persist	Stagnating score or score is less than 50% increase of the required rate
Paraguay	88	68.8	Major challenges persist	Moderate score improvement; score is insufficient for goal achievement
Suriname	92	68.3	Major challenges persist	Stagnating score or score is less than 50% increase of the required rate
Guyana	96	67.4	Major challenges persist	Moderate score improvement; score is insufficient for goal achievement
Panama	97	67.3	Major challenges persist	Moderate score improvement; score is insufficient for goal achievement
Nicaragua	104	64.8	Major challenges persist	Moderate score improvement; score is insufficient for goal achievement
Belize	107	64.6	Major challenges persist	Stagnating score or score is less than 50% increase of the required rate
Trinidad and Tobago	114	63.0	Challenges persist	Moderate score improvement; score is insufficient for goal achievement
Honduras	116	63.0	Major challenges persist	Moderate score improvement; score is insufficient for goal achievement
Venezuela (Bolivarian Republic of)	117	62.9	Major challenges persist	Stagnating score or score is less than 50% increase of the required rate
Bahamas, The	124	60.9	Significant challenges persist	Moderate score improvement; score is insufficient for goal achievement

(continued)

Table 1.6 (continued)

Country	*SDG rank*	*SDG score*	*Goal 3. Good health and well-being*	
			Dashboard	*Trend*
Guatemala	127	59.4	Major challenges persist	Moderate score improvement; score is insufficient for goal achievement
Haiti	152	52.6	Major challenges persist	Stagnating score or score is less than 50% increase of the required rate

Source Developed with data from Sachs et al. (2023)

ranged from 3.2 to 12.9 percent (CEPAL, 2020), which was and is insufficient given the variety of health risks in the region.

Epidemics are of particular concern in Latin America and the Caribbean; the region is considered highly vulnerable in relation to a series of epidemics, including "influenza, chikungunya, Zika, yellow fever, measles, diphtheria, cholera, mpox" and, of course, COVID-19 also continues to pose specific challenges (WHO, 2023a). Moreover, the region has also been demonstrating a significant decrease in vaccination which reverted previous progress by about three decades; the main reason was that the lockdown policies mandated during the COVID-19 pandemic, particularly between 2020 and 2021, resulted in many parents that could not take their less than one-year-old children to get vaccinated. As a result, about 2.7 million children did not receive all essential vaccines (WHO, 2023a). Further, poverty and health are interconnected (Chokshi, 2018), therefore, as long as the region continues to endure high levels of poverty and extreme poverty, hope for improvement in social health to a satisfactory standard is significantly diminished.

The eleventh Sustainable Development Goal is "Sustainable cities and communities" and has seven targets and fifteen indicators; it aims to "Make cities and human settlements inclusive, safe, resilient and sustainable" (UN, 2023d). Although there is not a goal specifically for adequate housing, there is one target that relates to housing: target 11.1 which establishes the need for "adequate, safe and affordable housing, and basic services and upgrade slums" by the year 2030; the target's indicator is the "proportion of urban population living in slums, informal settlements or inadequate housing" (UN, 2023d). Table 1.7 includes the SDG rank and score, as well as the current progress of target 11.1 of Goal 11 achievement and the countries' trends in its attainment. Six countries are excluded as there is insufficient data for the SDG rank (see Table 1.4). The data shows that this aspect is the most polarizing; that is, while there are five countries that have reached the target, there are also eight with major challenges and unavailable data.

Rajagopal, UN Special Rapporteur on the right to adequate housing, reported that on a global scale approximately 100 million people are homeless, and 1.6 billion do not have acceptable housing as well as basic services, which may increase by 1.4 billion within the next seven years, i.e., by 2030 (OHCHR, 2023). In 2022, there were approximately 120 million people living in inadequate or informal housing in Latin America and the Caribbean (López, 2022). In urban areas, about 98 percent had electricity, 95 percent had water, and 85 percent had sanitation, and in rural areas, approximately 90 percent had electricity, 83 percent had access to water and only 60 percent had sanitation (CEPAL, 2022); therefore, housing refers to: (1) having a roof over one's head, and (2) having an adequate house (i.e., one that is equipped with basic services). The reasons why so many do not have adequate housing are vast; issues range from elevated prices, unaffordable prices, inability to save, lack of access to credit (derived from a nonexistent credit history, not having formal employment, and/or it being denied because of socio-economic and racial profiling), as well as poor health, poverty, and extreme poverty.

As can be seen in the above data, despite the fact that the Human Development Index reveals that the region has relatively high human development, this seems to not be the case with poverty, social health, and housing as measured by the sustainable development goals in question. Moreover, the results pertaining to the sustainable development goals are also not entirely descriptive of other sources' data. There very well may be many reasons for this, however, the fact that there is insufficient and unavailable data, due to lack of reporting or the approachability of the goals, is likely an important contributor to discrepancies (López-Fernández et al., 2022). The fact remains, however, that the region is lagging in terms of sustainable development, as per the three analyzed variables though there are indications of improvements.

Latin American and Caribbean countries are reporting significant improvements of the related indicators of the social development goals and human development, however, there continue to be significant disparities and social injustice within and amongst the countries in the

Table 1.7 Sustainable development goal 11, target 11.1—adequate, safe, and affordable housing, and basic services and upgrade slums—in Latin America and the Caribbean

Country	*SDG rank*	*SDG score*	*Goal 11. Target 11.1 adequate, safe, and affordable housing*	
			Dashboard	*Trend*
Chile	30	78.2	Target has been achieved	Score is on track or maintaining SDG achievement
Uruguay	32	77.7	Target has been achieved	Score is on track or maintaining SDG achievement
Cuba	46	74.1	Challenges persist	Score is decreasing
Brazil	50	73.7	Challenges persist	Unavailable data
Argentina	51	73.7	Significant challenges persist	Unavailable data
Costa Rica	52	73.6	Target has been achieved	Score is on track or maintaining SDG achievement
Dominican Republic	62	72.1	Challenges persist	Score is stagnating
Peru	65	71.7	Major challenges persist	Unavailable data
El Salvador	73	70.7	Significant challenges persist	Score is decreasing
Ecuador	74	70.4	Major challenges persist	Unavailable data
Colombia	76	70.0	Challenges persist	Score is stagnating
Mexico	80	69.7	Significant challenges persist	Score is stagnating
Jamaica	82	69.6	Unavailable data	Unavailable data
Barbados	84	69.3	Target has been achieved	Score is on track or maintaining SDG achievement

(continued)

Table 1.7 (continued)

Country	*SDG rank*	*SDG score*	*Goal 11. Target 11.1 adequate, safe, and affordable housing*	
			Dashboard	*Trend*
Bolivia (Plurinational State of)	87	68.8	Major challenges persist	Unavailable data
Paraguay	88	68.8	Significant challenges persist	Moderate score improvement
Suriname	92	68.3	Significant challenges persist	Score is decreasing
Guyana	96	67.4	Challenges persist	Score is on track or maintaining SDG achievement
Panama	97	67.3	Target has been achieved	Score is on track or maintaining SDG achievement
Nicaragua	104	64.8	Major challenges persist	Unavailable data
Belize	107	64.6	Significant challenges persist	Score is stagnating
Trinidad and Tobago	114	63.0	Target has been achieved	Score is on track or maintaining SDG achievement
Honduras	116	63.0	Major challenges persist	Unavailable data
Venezuela (Bolivarian Republic of)	117	62.9	Major challenges persist	Unavailable data
Bahamas, The	124	60.9	Target has been achieved	Score is on track or maintaining SDG achievement

(continued)

Table 1.7 (continued)

Country	*SDG rank*	*SDG score*	*Goal 11. Target 11.1 adequate, safe, and affordable housing*	
			Dashboard	*Trend*
Guatemala	127	59.4	Major challenges persist	Score is stagnating
Haiti	152	52.6	Major challenges persist	Score is stagnating

Source Developed with data from Sachs et al. (2023)

region. Thus, human development and sustainable development are particular issues of concern in the region given its complex history as well as current social, economic, political, and environmental crises. As such, the above discussion is indicative of the many reasons why the countries in the region continue to be emerging markets or developing countries.

There have been a series of efforts made to combat poverty and extreme poverty and ensure social health and housing led by governments in Latin America and the Caribbean which include social welfare programs, education and healthcare improvements, and land reform initiatives, amongst others; however, progress has been slow and uneven. There are many reasons why they have not been entirely successful, such as deep-rooted disparities, structural violence, corruption, impunity, political instability, hierarchical social structures, complacency, limited resources, as well as resistance to change. Also, in many cases, time proves to be a significant deterrent as even when government leaders have sound proposals, the time they are in office is often not enough to see desired results. In other words, the region's sustainable development is still emerging, that is, specific efforts are made toward social well-being, however, they are currently still insufficient to account for sustained human development and deserved quality of life.

The first group of people in action in social enterprises were, then, unintentional contributors. Their actions and decisions inadvertently contributed to shaping the current state of affairs. Markedly, such events led to the need for organizations, specifically non-governmental organizations, with social strategic objectives, that is, social enterprises. It is not surprising that social entrepreneurship tends to emerge during particular periods in history (Light, 2009). Moreover, according to the United Nations General Assembly, social enterprises can "help to alleviate poverty and catalyse social transformation by strengthening the productive capacities of those in vulnerable situations and producing goods and services accessible to them" (UN General Assembly, 2023b, p. 1); as such, these enterprises can take action in relation to the work necessary to move toward the attainment of human development and sustainable development.

While the future cannot be assured, understanding historic events can provide substantial knowledge on how societies can evolve and the actions and decisions that must be taken today to generate different outcomes. The region's countries' particular limitations to adopt transformational policies lead to governments necessitating additional assistance to effectively shift from emerging to attained sustainable development; such assistance can certainly come from social enterprises. The next chapter discusses social enterprises and their pivotal role in driving positive societal change. Further, the historic events discussed also point to a particular need for collaboration and cooperation amongst interested parties, who are part of group three of people in action which will be discussed in Chapter 3.

References

Alqassim, A., & El-Setouhy. M. (2022). Impact of poverty on health. In A. E. Önal, (Ed.), *Healthcare access—new threats, new approaches*. https://doi.org/10.5772/intechopen.108704

Álvarez, D. B. C. (2016). La conquista y colonización española de América. *Historia Digital, XVI*(28), 103–149.

Amiune, J. M. (2021). *La invención de América Latina*. MERCOSUR ABC. Retrieved March 1st, 2024, from: https://www.mercosurabc.com.ar/la-invencion-de-america-latina

Ardisana, E. F. H., & Gaínza, B. M. (2022). Biodiversity, culture and bioeconomy in Latin America. *Revista Chakiñan de Ciencias Sociales y Humanidades, 18*, 203–212. https://doi.org/10.37135/chk.002.18.14

Arenas, J. O. (2005). *México, la dictadura perfecta*. Mexico: Coyoacán Editores. ISBN:9789709832006

Arpini, A. (2014). Nuestra América: la lucha por la significación. Francisco Bilbao y José Martí. *La Cañada.*, *5*, 182–201.

Arratia, A. (2010). Dictaduras latinoamericanas. *Revista Venezolana de Análisis de Coyuntura, XVI*(1), 33–51.

Azcona, G., & Bhatt, A. (2023). *Poverty is not gender-neutral*. SDG Action. Retrieved October 19th, 2023, from: https://sdg-action.org/poverty-is-not-gender-neutral/

Azcona, G., Bhatt, A., Brauchle, J., Fillo, G. F., Min, Y., Page, H., & Zhang, Y. (2022). *Progress on the sustainable development goals the gender snapshot*. UN Women and United Nations Department of Economic and Social Affairs, Statistics Division. Retrieved November 28th, 2023, from: https://www.unwomen.org/sites/default/files/2022-09/Progress-on-the-sustainable-development-goals-the-gender-snapshot-2022-en_0.pdf

Baah, S. K. T., Aguilar, R. A. C., Diaz-Bonilla, C., Fujs, T., Lakner, C., Nguyen, M. C., Viveros, M. (2023). *March 2023 global poverty update from the World Bank: the challenge of estimating poverty in the pandemic*. The World Bank. Retrieved October 15th, 2023, from: https://blogs.worldbank.org/opendata/march-2023-global-poverty-update-world-bank-challenge-estimating-poverty-pandemic

Banco Mundial. (2021). *Rompiendo barreras—Inclusión de las personas con discapacidad en América Latina y el Caribe*. Infografía. Retrieved June 6th, 2023, from: https://www.bancomundial.org/es/news/infographic/2021/12/03/rompiendo-barreras-inclusion-de-las-personas-con-discapacidad-en-america-latina-y-el-caribe

Barrantes, M. A. F. (1980). La herencia colonial de América Latina. *Revista Estudios, 2*(1), 51–60. https://doi.org/10.15517/re.v2i1.30969

Boisrobert, C. E., Stjepanovic, A., Oh, S., & Lelieveld, H. L. M. (2010). Chapter 2—Development of Food Legislation Around the World. Ensuring Global Food Safety. *Exploring Global Harmonization*. (pp. 5–69). https://doi.org/10.1016/B978-0-12-374845-4.00002-3

Bovarnick, A. & Alpizar, F. (2010). Chapter 1. Introduction. In A. Bovarnick, F. Alpizar, & C. Schnell, (Eds.), *Importance of biodiversity and ecosystems in economic growth and equity in Latin America and the Caribbean: An economic valuation of ecosystems. Latin America and the Caribbean: A Biodiversity Super Power* (pp. 2–5). New York: UNDP. Retrieved July 10th, 2023, from: https://www.undp.org/sites/g/files/zskgke326/files/publications/Report_ENG.pdf

Bovarnick, A., Alpizar, F., & Schnell, C. (2010). *Importance of biodiversity and ecosystems in economic growth and equity in Latin America and the Caribbean: An economic valuation of ecosystems. Latin America and the Caribbean: A Biodiversity Super Power*. New York: UNDP. Retrieved July 10th, 2023, from: https://www.undp.org/sites/g/files/zskgke326/files/publications/Report_ENG.pdf

Britanica. (2023). *Nicaragua*. Countries of the World. Retrieved August 5th, 2023, from: https://www.britannica.com/place/Nicaragua

Castañeda, C. F. B. (2019). La subjetividad en Latinoamérica y el Caribe desde visiones críticas de pensamiento contemporáneo. *Tla-melaua, 13*(46), 238–264. https://doi.org/10.32399/rtla.0.46.580

CEPAL. (2014). *Los pueblos indígenas en América Latina. Avances en el último decenio y retos pendientes para la garantía de sus derechos.* Santiago: United Nations. Retrieved October 1st, 2023 from: https://repositorio.cepal.org/server/api/core/bitstreams/b1b631f7-30df-4668-9047-6e2060cb30a6/content

CEPAL. (2019). *Panorama Social de América Latina 2019* (Santiago: Naciones Unidas, 2019), 259. Comisión Económica para América Latina y el Caribe. Retrieved August 10th, 2023, from: https://repositorio.cepal.org/server/api/core/bitstreams/d72d0e2f-76bb-4857-9a02-101784439750/content

CEPAL. (2020). *Gasto corriente total en salud como porcentaje del producto interno bruto.* CEPALSTAT Base de datos y Publicaciones Estadísticas. Retrieved October 1st, 2023, from.: https://statistics.cepal.org/portal/databank/index.html?lang=es&indicator_id=55&members=

CEPAL. (2022). *Hogares según disponibilidad de servicios básicos en la vivienda, por área geográfica.* CEPALSTAT Portal de desigualdades en América Latina. Retrieved November 30th, 2023, from: https://statistics.cepal.org/portal/inequalities/housing-and-basic-services.html?lang=es&indicator=260

CEPAL. (2023a). *Principales cifras de América Latina y el Caribe.* CEPALSTAT. Retrieved October 9th, 2023, from: https://statistics.cepal.org/portal/cepalstat/index.html?lang=es

CEPAL. (2023b). *Acerca. Comisión Económica para América Latina y el Caribe.* Retrieved August 2nd, 2023, from: https://www.cepal.org/es/acerca

Chokshi, D. A. (2018). Income, poverty, and health inequality. *Journal of the American Medical Association, 319*(13), 1312–1313. https://doi.org/10.1001/jama.2018.2521

CIA. (2023). *The World factbook.* Retrieved March 1st, 2024, from: https://www.cia.gov/the-world-factbook/countries/

Cruz-Martinez, G. (2019). Puerto Rico, colonialism and neocolonialism. In I. Ness & Z. Cope (Eds.), *The Palgrave encyclopedia of imperialism and anti-imperialism.* Palgrave Macmillan.

De Santos, A. L. (2021). *Todos estos territorios del mundo han sido en algún momento parte de España.* La Razón. Retrieved July 2nd, 2023, from: https://www.larazon.es/cultura/historia/20211124/52llo5ekvbdphlwmk3lu2ncqxm.html

Denevan, W. M. (1992). The pristine myth: The landscape of the Americas in 1942. *Annals of the Association of American Geographers, 82*(3), 369–385.

Department of State. (2009). *Grenada (10/06)*. Previous Editions of Grenada Background Note. Retrieved August 4th, 2023, from: https://2009-2017.state.gov/outofdate/bgn/grenada/74156.htm#:~:text=The%20Treaty%20of%20Paris%20formally,remainder%20of%20the%20colonial%20period.

DESA. (2023). *The 17 goals*. The United Nations Department of Economic and Social Affairs. Sustainable development. Retrieved March 10th, 2023, from: https://sdgs.un.org/goals

Dussel, E. (1967). *Hipótesis para una historia de la iglesia en América Latina*. Editorial Estela.

Emerging Money. (2012). *What is the difference between a developed, emerging, and frontier market?* NASDAQ. Retrieved June 4th, 2023, from: https://www.nasdaq.com/articles/what-difference-between-developed-emerging-and-frontier-market-2012-05-11

ESA. (2023). *History of French Guiana*. Europe's Spaceport. Retrieved August 3rd, 2023, from: https://www.esa.int/Enabling_Support/Space_Transportation/Europe_s_Spaceport/History_of_French_Guiana#:~:text=French%20Guiana%20has%20also%20been,made%20a%20French%20Overseas%20Department.

Fernandez, N.T. (2022). Chapter 12: The Caribbean: introducing the region. In K. Nelson, & N. T. Fernandez, (Eds.), *Gendered lives. Global issues*. New York: SUNY Press. Retrieved June 10th, 2023 from MILNE Library: https://milnepublishing.geneseo.edu/genderedlives/chapter/chapter-12-the-caribbean-introducing-the-region/#:~:text=The%20four%20main%20colonial%20powers,Portugal%2C%20Sweden%2C%20and%20Denmark

Fynn Bruey, V., & Crawley, H. (2024). The enduring impacts of slavery: A historical perspective on South-South migration. In H. Crawley & J. K. Teye (Eds.), *The Palgrave Handbook of South–South migration and inequality*. Palgrave Macmillan.

Gaiger, L. I. (2017). The solidarity economy in South and North America: Converging experiences. *Brazilian Political Science Review, 11*(3), 1–27. https://doi.org/10.1590/1981-3821201700030002

Gomes, R., Castilla, T., & Bertucci, J. (2012). *La economía solidaria en América Latina y el Caribe. Actores, presencia, experiencias, redes; reflexión y desafíos*. Retrieved March 30th, 2024, from: https://base.socioeco.org/docs/celam_dejusol_economia_solidaria_en_america_latina.pdf

Gruss, B., Nabar, M., Poplawski-Ribeiro, M. (2017). *Emerging Markets and Developing Economies: Sustaining growth in a less supportive external environment*. IMF. Emerging and frontier financial markets. Retrieved August 5th, 2023, from: https://www.imf.org/en/Blogs/Articles/2017/04/12/emergingmarketsanddevelopingeconomiessustaininggrowthinalesssupportiveexternal environment

Herrera, L. C. M. (2017). Proceso de Integración de América Latina y el Caribe. *Revista de Ciencias Sociales, IV*(158), 167–183. https://doi.org/10.15517/rcs.v0i158.32785

IFRC. (2023). *7 desastres en América en 2023 de los que quizá no hayas oído hablar*. Retrieved October 9th, 2023 from: https://www.ifrc.org/es/articulo/7-desastres-en-america-en-2023-los-que-quiza-no-hayas-oido-hablar

Kapoor, A., & Debroy, B. (2019). *GDP is not a measure of human well-being*. Harvard Business Review. Retrieved December 11th, 2023, from: https://hbr.org/2019/10/gdp-is-not-a-measure-of-human-well-being

Keller, S. (2016). *The age of exploration*. Britanica Educational Publishing.

Kliksberg, B. (2004). Diez falacias sobre los problemas sociales de América Latina. In M. E. B. Alvarado, & V. F. García, (Eds.), *La ilusión del buen gobierno. Sociedad civil, democracia y desarrollo humano en América Latina*. UNESCO–MOST.

Kline, H. F., Wade, C. J., & Wiarda, H. J. (2018). *Latin American politics and development*. Taylor & Francis. https://doi.org/10.4324/9780429495045

Kohn, M., & Reddy, K. (2017). Colonialism. In E. N. Zalta, & U. Nodelman, (Eds.), *The Stanford encyclopedia of philosophy*. Stanford University. Retrieved September 2nd, 2023 from: https://plato.stanford.edu/archives/fall2017/entries/colonialism/

Lange, M., & Dawson, A. (2009). Dividing and ruling the world? A statistical test of the effects of colonialism on postcolonial civil violence. *Social Forces, 88*(2), 785–817. https://doi.org/10.1353/sof.0.0255

Light, P. C. (2009). Social entrepreneurship revisited. *Stanford Social Innovation Review, 7*(3), 21–22. https://doi.org/10.48558/Z8K2-W870

López, P. (2022). *Banco de Desarrollo de América Latina y el Caribe*. Visiones. Retrieved August 11th, 2023, from: https://www.caf.com/es/conocimiento/visiones/2022/03/hacia-un-mejor-acceso-a-la-vivienda-en-america-latina-y-el-caribe/

López, J. C. B., Grajales, J. F. V., & Galeano, M. S. M. (2021). Dictatorships in Latin America and their influence of right and left movements since the 20th century. *Revista Ratio Juris, 16*(32), 17–50. https://doi.org/10.24142/raju.v16n32a1

López-Fernández, A. M., Terán-Bustamante, A., & Martínez-Velasco, A. (2022). Machine learning sustainable competitiveness for global recovery. In A. M. López-Fernández & A. Terán-Bustamante (Eds.), *Business recovery in emerging markets, Palgrave studies in democracy, innovation, and entrepreneurship for growth* (pp. 241–267). Palgrave Macmillan.

Mahoney, J. (2003). Long-run development and the legacy of colonialism in Spanish America. *American Journal of Sociology, 109*(1), 50–106. https://doi.org/10.1086/378454

Marañón-Pimentel, B., Caballero, H., González, S., Morales, F., & Moreno, G. (2020). *Descolonialidad del poder: sentipensares desde México*. Universidad Nacional Autónoma de México, Instituto de Investigaciones Económicas. https://doi.org/10.22201/iiec.9786073028813e.2020

Marichal, C. (2015). El nacimiento de los estudios internacionales sobre América Latina: Comentarios a las obras de José María Torres Caicedo y Carlos Calvo a mediados del siglo XIX. *Foro Internacional, 55*(3), 707–736.

Mark, J. J. (2020). *Colonización europea de las Américas*. World History Encyclopedia. Retrieved December 4th, 2023, from: https://www.worldhistory.org/trans/es/1-19230/colonizacion-europea-de-las-americas/#google_vignette

Montiel, P. J. (2011). *Macroeconomics in emerging markets*. Cambridge University Press.

Nohlen, D. (1993). *Enciclopedia Electoral Latinoamericana y del Caribe*. Instituto Interamericano de Derechos Humanos (IIDH). Universidad Nacional Autónoma de México. Instituto de Investigaciones Jurídicas. Retrieved May 24th, 2024, from: http://ru.juridicas.unam.mx/xmlui/handle/123456789/10966?show=full

Nyssens, M., Wanderley, F., & Gaiger, L. I. (2019). Introduction. Social enterprise in Latin America: Context and concepts. In L. I. Gaiger, M. Nyssens, & F. Wanderley (Eds.), *Social Enterprise in Latin America. Theory, models and practice* (pp. 1–26). Routledge.

Office of the Historian. (2023). *A Guide to the United States' History of Recognition, Diplomatic, and Consular Relations, by Country, since 1776: Saint Kitts and Nevis*. Countries. Retrieved August 4th, 2023, from: https://history.state.gov/countries/saint-kitts-nevis#:~:text=Present%2Dday%20Saint%20Kitts%20and,with%20Great%20Britain%20in%201967.

OHCHR. (2023). *UN expert urges action to end global affordable housing crisis*. The United Nations Human Rights Office of the High Commissioner Media Center. Retrieved October 22nd, 2023, from: https://www.ohchr.org/en/press-releases/2023/10/un-expert-urges-action-end-global-affordable-housing-crisis

OPS. (2023a). *Monitoreo de amenazas naturales*. Organización Panamericana de Salud. Retrieved October 9th, 2023, from: https://www.paho.org/es/emergencias-salud/monitoreo-amenazas-naturales

OPS. (2023b). *OPS y AIDS Healthcare Foundation colaborarán para eliminar el VIH/sida, la TB y otras infecciones en América Latina y el Caribe*. Noticias. Retrieved June 6th, 2023, from: https://www.paho.org/es/noticias/2-5-2023-ops-aids-healthcare-foundation-colaboraran-para-eliminar-vihsida-tb-otras

Peregalli, A., & Ochoa, E. (2023). Higher education and social engagement in Latin America. In R. Munck, Y. Pinilla, R. A. Hodges, & C. Bartch (Eds.),

Higher education in Latin America and the Caribbean Civic engagement and the democratic mission (pp. 60–77). Machdohnil Ltd.

Pinedo, J. (2015). Apuntes sobre el concepto postcolonialidad: Semejanzas y diferencias en su concepción y uso entre los intelectuales indios y latinamericanistas. *UNIVERSUM., 30*(1), 189–216.

Pozo, J. D. (2009). *Historia de América Latina y el Caribe. Desde la independencia hasta hoy*. LOM Ediciones.

Prado, A. (2021). *Emprendimiento Social en América Latina: Buenas prácticas para llevar productos y servicios a poblaciones rurales de escasos recursos.* INCAE Business School. Retrieved March 29th, 2023, from: https://cnnespanol.cnn.com/wp-content/uploads/2021/06/Reporte-Emprendimiento-Social-en-Ame%CC%81rica-Latina_Andrea-Prado-INCAE_VF.pdf

Quam, J., & Campbell, S. (2023). Chapter 77. Latin America and the Caribbean (LACAR): Historical Geography II—British Overseas Territories. *The western world: Daily readings on geography*. Pressbooks. Retrieved July 7th, 2023, from: https://cod.pressbooks.pub/westernworlddailyreadingsgeography/chapter/latin-america-and-the-caribbean-lacar-historical-geography-ii/

Radbound University. (2023). *Historical database Suriname Curaçao*. History. Retrieved August 7th, 2023, from: https://www.ru.nl/hdsc/history/

Rausch, J. M. (2016). Dictatorship in South America by Jerry Dávila (review). *The Latin Americanist, 60*(4), 592–593. https://doi.org/10.1111/tla.12098_8

Reyes, A. R. (2016). El giro decolonial en el siglo XXI. *Revista Ensayos Pedagógicos, 11*(2), 133–158. https://doi.org/10.15359/rep.11-2.6

Rojas Mix, M. (1986). Bilbao y el hallazgo de América latina: Unión continental, socialista y libertaria. *Cahiers Du Monde Hispanique Et Luso-Brésilien, 46*, 35–47.

Sachs, J.D., Lafortune, G., Fuller, G., & Drumm, E. (2023). *Sustainable Development Report 2023. Implementing the SDG Stimulus*. Paris: SDSN, Dublin: Dublin University Press. https://doi.org/10.25546/102924. Retrieved October 12th, 2023, from: https://s3.amazonaws.com/sustainabledevelopment.report/2023/sustainable-development-report-2023.pdf

Salazar-Xirinachs, J. M., García-Buchaca, R., & Sally Shaw, S. (2023). *Investment and cooperation opportunities for Latin America and the Caribbean and the European Union*. ECLAC. Retrieved August 28th, 2023, from: https://repositorio.cepal.org/server/api/core/bitstreams/54a2d6d4-9756-4937-b5ac-13b8b2e47eb2/content

San Martín, A. G. (2013). Francisco Bilbao, entre el proyecto latinoamericano y el gran molusco. *Latinoamérica. Revista de estudios Latinoamericanos*. 56, 141–162. https://www.scielo.org.mx/pdf/latinoam/n56/n56a7.pdf

Schwab, K. (2020). *Global Gender Gap Report 2020.* World Economic Forum. Retrieved October 21st, 2023, from: http://www3.weforum.org/docs/WEF_GGGR_2020.pdf

Singh, S. A. (2019). Indian indentured laborers in the Caribbean. In S. Ratuva (Ed.), *The Palgrave Handbook of Ethnicity.* Palgrave Macmillan.

Statista Research Department. (2023). *Most important problems faced by Latin America according to opinion leaders and journalists in 2022. Politics & Government.* Retrieved December 18th, 2023, from: https://www.statista.com/statistics/1069008/latin-america-main-problems/

Stern, S. J. (1985). Latin America's Colonial History: Invitation to an Agenda. Latin American Perspectives. *Latin America's Colonial History, 12*(1), 3–16. https://doi.org/10.1177/0094582X8501200010

The Permanent Mission of Saint Lucia. (2023). *History of Saint Lucia.* Retrieved August 3rd, 2023 From About Saint Lucia: http://saintluciamissionun.org/about-saint-lucia/

The World Bank. (2001). *World Development Report 2000/2001: Attacking Poverty.* Washington, Oxford University Press. Retrieved September 14th, 2023, from: https://documents1.worldbank.org/curated/en/230351468332946759/pdf/226840WDR00PUB0ng0poverty0200002001.pdf

The World Bank. (2022a). *Understanding poverty.* Retrieved September 9th, 2023 from: https://www.worldbank.org/en/understanding-poverty

The World Bank. (2022b). *Poverty. Overview.* Understanding Poverty. Retrieved October 15th, 2023, from: https://www.worldbank.org/en/topic/poverty/overview

UN. (2015). *News on Millennium Development Goals.* Retrieved September 20th, 2023 from: https://www.un.org/millenniumgoals/

UN. (2023a). *Regional groups of Member States. Department for General Assembly and Conference Management.* Retrieved March 1st, 2024, from: https://www.un.org/dgacm/en/content/regional-groups

UN. (2023b). *Goal 1. End poverty in all its forms everywhere.* The United Nations Department of Economic and Social Affairs. Sustainable Development. Retrieved September 10th, 2023, from: https://sdgs.un.org/goals/goal1#targets_and_indicators

UN. (2023c). *Goal 3. Good health and well-being.* The United Nations Department of Economic and Social Affairs Sustainable Development. Retrieved August 4th, 2023, from: https://sdgs.un.org/goals/goal3

UN. (2023d). *Goal 11. Sustainable cities and communities.* The United Nations Department of Economic and Social Affairs. Sustainable Development. Retrieved September 10th, 2023, from: https://sdgs.un.org/goals/goal11#overview

UN General Assembly. (2023a). *Extreme poverty in developing countries inextricably linked to global food insecurity crisis, Senior Officials tell Second*

Committee. Seventy-eighth session, 16th & 17th meetings (am & pm). Retrieved October 14th, 2023 from: https://press.un.org/en/2023/gaef3590.doc.htm

UN General Assembly. (2023b). Resolution A/77/L.60. Promoting the social and solidarity economy for sustainable development. Retrieved May 9th, 2024, from: https://documents.un.org/doc/undoc/ltd/n23/086/72/pdf/n2308672.pdf?token=ByCtww4PCMdy0z4X8w&fe=true

UNSDG. (2018). *Challenges and strategies for sustainable development in Latin America and the Caribbean*. The Sustainable Development Group of the United Nations. Retrieved April 18th, 2023, from: https://unsdg.un.org/sites/default/files/Challenges-and-Strategies-for-Sustainable-Development-in-Latin-America-and-the-Caribbean.pdf

UNDP. (2022). *Human development Index*. Human Development Reports. Retrieved October 30th, 2023, from: https://hdr.undp.org/data-center/human-development-index#/indicies/HDI

UNDP. (2023a). *What are the Sustainable Development Goals*? The SDGs in action. Retrieved September 20th, 2023, from: https://www.undp.org/sustainable-development-goals

UNDP. (2023b). *165 million people fell into poverty between 2020 to 2023 as debt servicing crowded out social protection, health and education expenditures*. News Center. Retrieved October 15th, 2023, from: https://www.undp.org/press-releases/165-million-people-fell-poverty-between-2020-2023-debt-servicing-crowded-out-social-protection-health-and-education-expenditures

UNDRR. (2023). *Overview of disasters in Latin America and the Caribbean 2000–2022*. Retrieved October 23rd, 2023 from; https://www.undrr.org/media/89900/download?startDownload=20240825

UNICEF. (2023). *Children bearing brunt of stalled progress on extreme poverty reduction worldwide*. Retrieved October 15th, 2023 from: https://www.unicef.org/press-releases/children-bearing-brunt-stalled-progress-extreme-poverty-reduction-worldwide

United Nations. (1987). *Report of the World Commission on Environment and Development*. United Nations Digital Library. Retrieved May 9th, 2023, from: https://digitallibrary.un.org/record/139811?ln=en

United Nations. (2023). *The Sustainable Development Goals Report 2023: Special edition towards a rescue plan for people and planet*. Retrieved December 1st 2023 from: https://unstats.un.org/sdgs/report/2023/The-Sustainable-Development-Goals-Report-2023.pdf

United Nations High Commissioner for Human Rights. (2022). *Racism, discrimination are legacies of colonialism*. Retrieved October 9th, 2023, from: https://www.ohchr.org/en/get-involved/stories/racism-discrimination-are-legacies-colonialism#:~:text=Cal%C3%AD%20Tzay%20added%20that%20the,of%20language%20and%20culture%2C%20and

Victoriano Serrano, F. (2010). Estado, golpes de Estado y militarización en América Latina: Una reflexión histórico política. *Argumentos, 23*(64), 175–193.

Vilaboy, S. G. (1997). Etapas y procesos en la historia de América Latina. *Cuadernos de trabajo.* Instituto de investigaciones Histórico-Sociales. Veracruz: Universidad Veracruzana. Retrieved October 13th, 2023 from: https://biblioteca.clacso.edu.ar/Mexico/iih-s-uv/20170608043740/pdf_473.pdf

WHO. (2023a). *WHO's Health Emergency Appeal, 2023.* Retrieved October 16th, 2023 from: https://iris.who.int/bitstream/handle/10665/365635/WHO-WHE-EXR-2023.1-eng.pdf?sequence=1

WHO. (2023b). *WHO remains firmly committed to the principles set out in the preamble to the Constitution.* Constitution. Retrieved July 18th, 2023, from: https://www.who.int/about/accountability/governance/constitution

WHO. (2024). *Human development index.* Retrieved March 7th, 2024 from: https://www.who.int/data/nutrition/nlis/info/human-development-index#:~:text=The%20HDI%20is%20a%20summary,knowledge%20and%20standard%20of%20living.

World Economic Forum. (2023). *Global Gender Gap Report 2023.* Reports. Retrieved September 21st, 2023 from: https://www.weforum.org/publications/global-gender-gap-report-2023/digest/

WPP. (2022). *Definition of Regions. Population Divisions.* UN World Population Prospects 2022. Retrieved March 1st, 2024, from: https://population.un.org/wpp/DefinitionOfRegions/#:~:text=Geographic%20regions%3A%20countries%20and%20areas,%3B%20Northern%20America%2C%20and%20Oceania.

Ypi, L. (2016). Qué está mal con el colonialismo. *Signos Filosóficos, 18*(36), 140–176.

CHAPTER 2

Social Enterprises: Profit for Social Development

Abstract Latin America and the Caribbean is diverse, growing, and also one of the most unequal and turbulent regions making slow progress toward human and sustainable development. Each country's reality presents particular needs which are not met, and cannot solely be met, by their governments; for such matter, social enterprises are not only important but are strategic to achieve social growth and development. Business models, leadership, and approach to profit with purpose are elemental for creating a responsible social enterprise, for effective operation, performance, and success.

Keywords Social enterprise · Sociopreneurs · Leadership · Profit with purpose · Triple-bottom-line · Hybridity · Social entrepreneurship · Shared value · Social enterprise responsibility

Emerging markets and developing countries, such as those in Latin America and the Caribbean, are in a constant uphill battle for growth and development. For such reasons, social enterprises have taken on a particularly key role in not only alleviating the burden of what most would consider to be governments' responsibilities, but also in enhancing social well-being as well as environmental sustainability. Despite the fact

A. M. López-Fernández, *Co-Creation in Social Enterprises*, Palgrave Studies of Entrepreneurship and Social Challenges in Developing Economies, https://doi.org/10.1007/978-3-031-83449-3_2

that social enterprises have been operating for hundreds of years and the number of these organizations is growing globally, it is common to mistake them as organizations with traditional business models that merely have social intentions. In fact, searching for social enterprises may yield results of a series of organizations that state to be engaged in social responsibility or are invested in green practices, rather than social enterprises or social entrepreneurships. This not only causes a conceptual issue, but also makes it more difficult for interested parties or potential stakeholders to understand their role in social enterprises' performance, and social and environment development. Therefore, social entrepreneurs may find it difficult to achieve a desired degree of public engagement with its strategic objectives and operations.

Leadership, as a function of management, is elemental to the effective operation and success of any organization which, of course, includes social enterprises. The second group of people in action in social enterprises are their leaders, founders, and CEOs; this chapter discusses the designers and architects of social enterprises. To begin, this chapter goes back in time to understand the origins and creation of social enterprises followed by a discussion on their definition and the different associated theories. The main attributes of social enterprise leaders are analyzed in relation to the organization's performance. Then, the characteristics of the profit-with-purpose approach to business are described as well as the four main ways in which it is managed. Finally, examples of social enterprises' impact on poverty, social health, and housing, are explored.

It is fair to say that human beings have always struggled with issues impeding growth and development in varying degrees, including, but not limited to: predators, diseases, environmental change, injury, housing, political risk, inequity, financial and economic crises, social injustice, structural violence, hunger, and poverty. The reality is that, although these and many more issues have affected societies worldwide, those living in developing countries and emerging markets have been far more afflicted than those in developed countries; reasons range from negative economic growth, recession, corruption, impunity, and lack of infrastructure to political instability and conflict, amongst others. Effectively addressing these issues is complex and, thus, would require the cooperation of both public and private organizations. Therefore, the national and international interest in continuous efforts to alleviate such issues in order to achieve growth and development globally is not only reasonable but also necessary.

Discussions and debates about organizations' responsibility toward society and how they should go about defining, designing, and executing objectives and strategies to do so, have persisted for decades amongst scholars, researchers, and practitioners. Some argue that business' responsibilities start and end with the business, and others posit that responsibilities should extend beyond business operations. Further, while big business tends to catch a reputation of doing what is necessary to turn a profit, usually done by turning a blind eye to the negative impact of their operations on society and the environment, there is centuries of evidence of businesspeople making decisions that favor societal well-being; in such a way that social enterprises, organizations with a dual mission and responsibility, and those taking a profit-with-purpose approach, are not a modern notion, practice, or business model; however, they have certainly become much more prominent in recent decades (British Council, 2022).

There are many ways in which organizations have attempted to reduce the negative effects of their decisions and operations on society and the environment, as well as to tackle a variety of issues that have been pervading society and the environment seemingly unrelated to their decisions and operations. The most prominent being social responsibility (SR) or corporate social responsibility (CSR), social entrepreneurship or social enterprises, as well as social businesses. Although they have different characteristics and entail somewhat different approaches to business, there are certain aspects where they intersect or converge. For instance, they all center around the notion that societies deserve a certain standard of living that enhances their quality of life, and the environment should not be haphazardly made use of, let alone exploited. Despite the similarities, it is important to analyze social enterprises as separate entities in order to fully understand the implications of said convergence.

Social Enterprises' Associated Theories

A little over a decade ago, the concept of social entrepreneurship was still in its early stages of development, and research continues to shape our understanding of its effects around the world. Therefore, there are many theories that have been associated with entrepreneurship, stemming from various fields of research and practice, such as psychology, sociology, management, and economics, amongst others. One of the most prominent, due to its seminal characteristic, is Schumpeter's (1934) theory of economic development. His theory posited the importance of the role of entrepreneurship in economic growth; entrepreneurs drive innovation, associated with products, processes, and business models and are, therefore, catalysts for disruption. They not only find ways to utilize inventions but also seek to enhance the recognition of opportunities by leveraging their intellectual capital to optimize potential business growth. Dees and Anderson (2006) suggest that social entrepreneurship is best understood when combining both social enterprise and social innovation schools of thought and practice; that is, enterprising social innovations. The latter proposes that these organizations are able to embrace social objectives and missions in an innovative manner. Although not all social enterprises revolve around an innovation, theorizing social enterprises in such a way prompts the notion of the generation of social value by means of creativity, resilience, flexibility, and of course innovativeness, to enhance social well-being. That being said, there is not a single theory that describes social enterprises' actions and behavior, in fact, there are many theories that may intersect or converge in the behavior of social enterprises as well as their leaders, including, but not limited to: the triple-bottom-line, hybridity, social entrepreneurship, stakeholder theory, and shared value, amongst others.

The behavioral theory of social enterprise suggests that social and business value may be created in unison through the organization's designed and executed strategic objectives, strategies, and tactics. That is, the co-creation of value is plausible by fostering synergy amongst the associated stakeholders, and aligning the organization's corporate philosophy, culture, and governance. Elkington (1997) coined the term triple-bottom-line, also known as TBL, which suggests that an organization's responsibilities should go beyond financial performance and include the 3Ps, these being: people (social), planet (environmental), and profit (financial), in order to be sustainable as well as remain sustainable. Social entrepreneurship has many commonalities with entrepreneurship; the most relevant being that it encompasses the attributes of both concepts, i.e., social and entrepreneurship. Therefore, social entrepreneurship is an entrepreneurial business which stems from a social initiative and purpose, and a motivation to generate sustainable solutions (Austin et al., 2006; Santos, 2012); social entrepreneurship theory is, then, consequential to social development (El Ebrashi, 2013).

Stakeholder theory, which is further analyzed in Chapter 3, refers to the enterprise's concern with and consideration of all interested parties' needs and wants to ensure a successful outcome (Freeman, 1984), or the organization's desired performance. Hybrid organizational theory refers to the balance of social and environmental value with financial value (Doherty et al., 2014). The technicality of the theory lies in ensuring that strategic objectives and efforts related to financial value do not take over as a priority over those related to social value. And shared value occurs when organizations work toward attaining financial gains that, in turn, generate benefits for society (Kramer & Pfitzer, 2016). Therefore, social enterprise behavior may take on the characteristics of any of the previous theories, or a combination of them, which is observed in the variety of the construct's definitions.

Defining Social Enterprises

The evolution of the term—social enterprise—has been correlated with the development of associated theories as well as changes in the environment. Determining the precise moment in history when social enterprises were created is difficult, to say the least, as these types of organizations have been present for centuries in various forms. For instance, according to the International Cooperative Alliance (2018), one of the first Cooperatives dates back to 1761 in Scotland. There is also a history of mutual aid societies, such as the *Mutualistas*, a Mexican American mutual aid society created in Los Angeles, dating back to the nineteenth and twentieth centuries (Condes, 2021), as well as other community focused and led organizations. However, there is also evidence of social enterprise activity dating back to the seventeenth century (MacDonald & Howorth, 2018); meaning that, the idea that businesspeople have a certain degree of responsibility toward society and/or interest in creating solutions for a social problem and the fact that they act on such notions, is not contemporary at all. In fact, business responsibility toward society has existed, to some degree, ever since the first businesses were created. That being said, while the concept of entrepreneurship became prevalent in economic works during the eighteenth century (Dueñas & Cedeño, 2020), the modern use of the social entrepreneurship and social enterprise concepts became widespread in the late twentieth and early twenty-first centuries (MacDonald & Howorth, 2018; Portales & Pérez, 2015), in fact, some attribute the first use of the term social entrepreneurship to Drayton, Ashoka founder and CEO, in the 1980s (Light, 2009).

Entrepreneurial organizations are usually small, innovative, and willing to take risks, and they drive economic growth by developing different approaches to business (Lederman et al., 2014; Rufer et al., 2021). Entrepreneurship in Latin America and the Caribbean is not all that different from other regions. In some cases, minor differences relate to the motives for entrepreneurship. For instance, Aguirre Quezada and Flores Muñoz (2018) have posited that a large number of organizations in the region, about 85 percent, are considered family owned/run enterprises and, therefore, tend to be created with the main purpose of satisfying a particular need as opposed to being driven by a business opportunity. According to Dueñas and Cedeño (2020), there are two main reasons for entrepreneurship, the first due to market opportunities or innovative initiatives to make a difference in and for society, and the second due to need, that is, as a means of survival given faced adversities.

Entrepreneurship in the region has a significant impact on economic growth, being positive in the countries with greater development; the countries with lower levels of development might see a lower or negative impact on economic growth which is an indicator that something may be executed incorrectly (Aguirre Quezada & Flores Muñoz, 2018). Despite common perception, formality of entrepreneurial organizations is not the main issue in Latin America and the Caribbean, rather a particular weakness associated with lack of innovation of processes and products (Lederman et al., 2014), in addition to scarce resources.

In terms of entrepreneurial activity in the early stages, there are entrepreneurs in Latin America that start their business with the intention of making a difference in the world, including 42.7 percent in Ecuador, 48.5 percent in Colombia, 57.6 percent in Chile, 62.8 percent in México, 68 percent in Panama, 68.4 percent in Venezuela, 69.3 percent in Puerto Rico, 76.5 percent in Brazil, and 80.6 percent in Guatemala (GEM, 2023). Therefore, there are many entrepreneurs in the region striving to create organizations, products, and/or services with a positive impact on well-being; in other words, those that can be aligned with the aims of social enterprises.

Mair and Martí (2006) view social entrepreneurship as a subgroup of entrepreneurship. Social entrepreneurship entails tackling local issues through social innovations as well as organizational frameworks (Portales & Pérez, 2015). Bonnici et al. (2024) posit that it is a process that tackles social issues through entrepreneurship practices. There is a lack of agreement on the conceptualization of social entrepreneurship in Latin America and the Caribbean as research remains in its early stages (García et al., 2020). However, social entrepreneurships in the region tend to be not-for-profit organizations operating with the objective to positively impact social development (Dueñas & Cedeño, 2020). Some consider social entrepreneurship and social enterprises synonymous, or elements of each other. For instance, according to Robinson (2006, p. 96), social entrepreneurship encompasses "social enterprises, social venture capital, and social purpose organizations"; in such a way that basically all organizations with a social purpose or mission may be included. Others make a distinction between both concepts; according to Del Cerro (2016), while social entrepreneurship entails launching a project with the aim of providing innovative solutions of social and/or environmental problems, social enterprises are essentially self-sustaining organizations that aim to generate a positive and measurable social and/or environmental impact.

Defourny and Nyssens (2010) suggest that social entrepreneurship and social enterprises relate to the context in which they emerge and are influenced by social, cultural, economic, and political characteristics. Luke and Chu (2013) have posited that social enterprises focus on their reason for existence, purpose, and social entrepreneurships focus on innovative processes that lead to the achievement of their social purpose. The fact of the matter is that social enterprises may operate like entrepreneurial organizations as well as take on aspects of entrepreneurship behavior theory. Having said that, the concept of social enterprise has been defined in various manners and, therefore, does not have a single definition, which could be related to the fact that these organizations are diverse, in terms of their structure, core operations, as well as target market (Shaw & Carter, 2007) and audience.

According to the Organization for Economic Cooperation and Development (OCDE), social enterprises are "organised with an entrepreneurial strategy whose main purpose is not the maximisation of profit but the attainment of certain economic and social goals, and which has the capacity for bringing innovative solutions to the problems of social exclusion and unemployment" (OECD, 1999). As such, it is generally accepted that social enterprises have the potential to create a social and environmental impact by developing solutions that are sustainable and positively affect interested parties. They operate in different sectors and create social value in an innovative manner (Austin, 2006); in such a way that social enterprises may be understood as a process by which either a problem or opportunity to solve the problem, as well as the potential effect on social development are identified and subsequently devised into the organization's business model to achieve its purpose (Robinson, 2006).

Social enterprises, which are "for-purpose organizations" (Hisyam & Lin, 2023, p. 1), vary in size, scope of operation, and mission. In terms of size, dynamic entrepreneurs in Latin America tend to lead medium and large enterprises which are also those with greater innovativeness (Lederman et al., 2014). These organizations tackle social issues or problems with business models (De Beule et al., 2023), which are commonly associated with entrepreneurial and other for-profit organizations; in such a way that the social aspects that lay at the center of their operations are tackled by means of a commercial-based business model, and the main difference is the social mission of the social enterprise. According to During (2016) social enterprises have the potential to influence and make significant social changes. They can do so by tackling social issues through products and services (Mair & Martí, 2006). Moreover, although their objectives are social and financial value (Short et al., 2009), the latter is consequential of the former (Prado, 2021).

Social enterprises are commonly considered to be part of the third sector, that is, the sector that is neither private nor public, yet considered a nonprofit private sector (Levy, 1996). Anheier (2001) posits that the third sector operates between the state and the market. Corry (2010) establishes that there is a difference in the perspective and definition of the third sector in terms of an American and European view; the former includes organizations that are voluntary, private, and not-for-profit, while the latter entails organizations such as associations, not-for-profit organizations, cooperatives, mutuals, and charities, amongst others, which may work with other sectors, i.e.: state and market. The Latin American view in general includes organizations that are not-for-profit that pursue public interests (Thompson, 2001) to enhance development and, thus, quality of life. Specifically, the third sector may include social enterprises, community groups and organizations, voluntary organizations, charities, cooperatives, housing associations, not-for-profit, and non-governmental organizations (Bowen, 2013a; Improvement and Development Agency, 2008; Northern Bridge, 2023), amongst others. That being said, Halsall et al. (2022) have argued that as social enterprises do not operate in single sector, and are hybrid, it is not possible to classify them in a particular sector. Meaning that they may operate within several sectors either simultaneously or by project.

Even though some authors have posited that social entrepreneurships are not-for-profit (Fowler, 2000), they can have many types of structures, such as for-profit, nonprofit, public (Prado, 2021), and private. Thus, social enterprises do not necessarily follow a typical structure of for-profit organizations, as their structure is shaped around the nature of their core business (Barrera Duque, 2007), which means that they cannot simply be viewed and analyzed by their business model (During, 2016); however, this does not mean that they are exempt from having a successful business model; that is, social enterprises are just like other businesses in that they are managed akin to a typical business, they may offer products and/or services to a market and, thus, endure costs and have an income (Yunus, 2010).

Traditional business models, usually associated with for-profit enterprises, are considered to be the models by which organizations generate profit by delivering value to consumers who are willing to pay for such value (Teece, 2010). There are certainly business models that generate profit but are not developed with said purpose; for instance, sustainable business models deliver value deriving from financial, social, and environmental performance (Preghenella & Battistella, 2021). Sustainable innovation business models converge sustainable innovation with financial performance (Boons & Wagner, 2009) in order to create and deliver value to their consumers. A particular difference between social enterprises' business models and conventional business models is that the latter seek to achieve the highest possible profit margin, and the former work toward remaining in the market and being competitive by covering their costs (Osorio-Novela et al., 2021). With this in mind, the products and/or services that they provide do create income, and given the variance of the latter, these enterprises tend to also utilize other resources (Gaiger et al., 2019) to achieve their strategic objectives. Such additional resources may include in-kind supplies, sources and materials, donations, grants, pro-bono expertise and consulting, volunteership, as well as commercial alliance participation, amongst others.

Although social enterprises can be of all sizes, most are classified as small and medium enterprises (SMEs) or micro, small, and medium enterprises (MSMEs) (Singh et al., 2012). While many may discard these organizations due to their size, it is important to remember that they make up the majority of organizations across industries; over a decade ago, about 90 percent of organizations around the world were MSMEs (Vandenberg, 2009), and today they account for approximately 99 percent of organizations (CEPAL, 2023). The size enables, amongst other aspects, their decision-making to be more flexible, intuitive, creative, and innovative, mostly because they are not constrained by bureaucratic processes, overhead, and an overall system of control focused more on checks and balances than the process of growth and development. Despite the fact that there is a significant percentage that perishes fairly quickly, they are particularly resilient, especially when considering the fact that most have little to no external investments and limited capital and resources.

The number of social enterprises has increased throughout the years (Noya, 2014), becoming a global phenomenon; in fact, according to the British Council (2022), there are approximately eleven million social enterprises around the world. However, Lepoutre et al. (2013), found that there is more social enterprise activity ensuing in countries in Africa and Latin America and the Caribbean. This makes sense as these regions include countries in which there are significantly more needs, greater areas of opportunity, less access to resources, obsolete institutions, greater disparity, and limited infrastructures, amongst others. Further, they also have a significantly larger portion of the population that is vulnerable and marginalized; therefore, in need of greater assistance to promote social well-being. Further, in 2023, the region's new entrepreneurs were responsible for greater job creations; for instance, according to the Global Entrepreneurship Monitor, "Puerto Rico, Chile, Brazil and Mexico each had more than three in 10 of those starting and running new businesses expecting to employ at least another six people over the next five years" (GEM, 2023, p. 18). This indicates that the interest in developing social enterprises and working with them has been growing.

Social Enterprise Leaders

The second group of people in action in social enterprises are social entrepreneurs; they are founders and leaders of the enterprises. They take action at different stages of organizational growth. Their first actions relate to creating the enterprise; they design the structure, philosophy, business model, governance, culture, etc. Then, their actions relate to strategic management and decision-making; importantly, their actions are associated with their leadership, both of the enterprise and their collaborators. Leadership is a function of management that can be described as a person's ability to influence others' behavior to achieve objectives; said ability is backed by their degree and use of power, authority, and influence. As such, leadership is elemental to effective performance regardless of the type of organization, size, or core business.

The style of leadership will significantly impact the organization's results as it is directly correlated with the organization's structure, degree and type of collaboration, decision-making, flexibility, and innovation. It also directly influences the design and execution of the organization's corporate philosophy, culture, governance, and stance on its responsibility toward society. The taxonomy of leadership styles is vast and diverse; there are generic forms, such as democratic, bureaucratic, and autocratic, as well as more specific, such as transformational, charismatic, transactional, and ethical, amongst many others. The way that organizational leaders envision organizational behavior is telling of the style of leadership that will, most likely, be adopted throughout the organization. Furthermore, leaders are only successful when their collaborators are receptive to their style of management.

Democratic styles of leadership are generally associated with social enterprise leaders. The World Economic Forum and the Schwab Foundation for Social Entrepreneurship developed a study and found that the majority of social entrepreneurs tend to be ethical, empowering, and transformational, as opposed to autocratic (Heinecke et al., 2014). These results make sense since ethical leadership entails operating on the basis of stipulated standards and what is considered to be appropriate behavior (Brown et al., 2005). Ethical leaders are not only trusted but are also considered to be fair and honest (Brown & Treviño, 2006), as they emphasize ethical decision-making (Zhu et al., 2014) throughout their operations. Therefore, at least the legal standard of ethics, meaning the local, national, and international laws and regulations, is considered within the organization's governance, processes, and procedures.

Transformational leaders are inspirational and motivational (Bass, 1990); they work with their collaborators as opposed to having collaborators that work for them, therefore, they are participatory. That is, they bring collaborators into the fold by making them aware of the relevance of the organization's intended results on the basis of their corporate philosophy and motivating them to actively participate in strategic decision-making processes. Thus, this style of leadership is well associated with structures that tend to the horizontal, decentralized decision-making, creativity, flexibility, innovation, proactive engagement, empowerment, effective stakeholder management, satisfaction, productivity, performance, and loyalty.

The term entrepreneur was included in the French dictionary, *Dictionnaire de la Langue Française*, in 1437; it was defined as: "a person who is active and gets things done" (Landström, 1999, p. 9). Over the years, the term has expanded to include a series of associated traits, skills, and competencies. According to Hisyam and Lin (2023, p. 1), social enterprises are led by "sociopreneurs". The main difference between entrepreneurs and social entrepreneurs is associated with their general objectives; the former's objectives are related to their interests and profit enhancement, and the latter are generally focused on social objectives (Vidovic, 2023). The reason(s) to take on a leadership role in social enterprises may be explained by social entrepreneurial intention; that is, an individual's thought process that leads to creating a plan (Gupta & Bhawe, 2007), to develop a social enterprise (Tran & Von Korflesch, 2016). They may have a vision of an organization that aims to serve a community facing a social issue, and/or see an opportunity in the environment for an innovative solution to a social problem. In both cases, they work toward a positive impact on social growth and development. There are various authors who have put forth a series of characteristics or traits associated with social entrepreneurs; Fig. 2.1 includes a word cloud with some of the concepts most commonly associated with social enterprise leaders.

According to the World Economic Forum and the Schwab Foundation for Social Entrepreneurship, about 76 percent of social entrepreneurs are between 42 and 65 years old, almost 90 percent are founders, and fifty percent are responsible for hiring between 26 and 100 people (Heinecke et al., 2014). In Latin America and the Caribbean, almost half of entrepreneurs, about 42 percent, are women and social entrepreneurs have higher education levels than other entrepreneurs (Prado, 2021). Moreover, in 2021, it was found that 40 percent of social entrepreneurs were responsible for generating over five jobs, which is not only relevant for the countries' growth but also impacts their collaborators and their families' well-being which, in turn, impacts financial and economic growth; 63 percent of social entrepreneurs also encouraged volunteership, and 67 percent stated that they expected the organization to grow (Prado, 2021).

Social enterprise leaders take action by innovatively tackling critical social or environmental issues (Del Cerro, 2016); by doing so,

Fig. 2.1 Social enterprise leaders' most common characteristics

they are able to generate benefits for society as well as maintain them (Mair & Noboa, 2006). In addition to being innovative, they have an entrepreneurial spirit and are focused on developing a business idea and goal achievement (Monguí Pintenel, 2023). Furthermore, successful sociopreneurs are those who are able to transform their ideas into profitable projects (Lederman et al., 2014), organizations, and/or solutions. The latter is achieved as they seek to promote and/or produce social output associated with society's well-being, health, as well as welfare (Leadbeater, 1997).

They are determined and driven by a passion that motivates and guides the enterprise's social mission (Dees, 1998). Similarly to non-social entrepreneurs, they are businesspeople; much like other types of organizations may develop their mission based on a product or service that they have developed to fill a need in the marketplace, social enterprises equally fill a need in the community and society. It makes sense, then, that social entrepreneurs are ethical and transformational; in addition, it is noteworthy that they also have good negotiation skills, as well as tact and diplomacy; this is particularly true for the leaders who tackle social and environmental issues by bridging the private and public sectors with their operations. As such, sociopreneurs' style of leadership has a direct effect on the organization's performance; therefore, their leadership impacts its growth (Koryak et al., 2015) and development.

According to Vasconcelos et al. (2022), the main indicators of social entrepreneurs' behavior include "entrepreneurial self-efficacy, social support, previous experience, moral obligation and empathy" (p. 177). They have a clear vision that integrates financial and social objectives in their business model, are particularly proficient at drumming up and managing resources, as well as successfully influencing others' actions toward goal achievement (Steinerowski & Steinerowska-Streb, 2012). These characteristics enable social entrepreneurs to advocate for and achieve social change (Borzaga et al., 2020).

Social entrepreneurs, or sociopreneurs, are able to draw attention to the needs of a certain sector or community of the country's population or environment on the basis of their experience and context; such need, in turn, informs or motivates the reason for existence of the organization itself. Then, their leadership style enables them to effectively manage the attainment of their social mission, whether related to tending to social issues, such as poverty, health, housing, and/or environmental problems; this can be performed especially well when their style is more democratic and transformational. Some examples of social enterprises in the region tackling social and environmental issues are discussed in the last section of this chapter. Table 2.1 includes some specific traits that are commonly associated with social enterprise leaders and their attainment of desired performance:

The positive characteristics of social entrepreneurs are not, and have not been, a guarantee for the success of social enterprises in Latin America and the Caribbean. While some oversights are related to the restrictions of the context, as per the region's current and historical context,

Table 2.1 Common social enterprise leaders' traits

• Adaptability	• Deference	• Participation
• Awareness	• Delegation	• Passion
• Collaboration	• Empathy	• Person-centric
• Communication	• Empowerment	• Problem solving
• Conflict resolution	• Engagement	• Resilience
• Cooperation	• Flexibility	• Result oriented
• Creativity	• Innovation	• Self-awareness

others derive from the lack of understanding of market and environmental dynamics. Despite the fact that entrepreneurs tend to embrace adversity and risk, some find it difficult to adapt to turbulent environments, and specific feedback from the community they serve. In other cases, mistakes occur due to a lack of strategic management or mismanagement; this may be caused by insufficient education or inability to execute effectively, which result in missed opportunities.

Some of the most common areas of opportunity include lack of professionalization, misalignment of the elements of the enterprise's philosophy, non-strategic planning, inadequate control systems, and ineffective financial management. They may not be able to provide products or services that satisfy the community's needs given their failure to understand and respond to market dynamics and/or cultural attributes and ignoring cues in the environment may impede potential partnerships and scalability. Further, the personal well-being of the entrepreneur is also an important factor. It is easy to prioritize work, especially when it is passion-driven, over physical, mental, and emotional well-being, which can lead to the social entrepreneur's burnout. All of the above impede social entrepreneurs from fulfilling their missions and objectives. And, tackling these shortcomings requires a blend of self-awareness, local knowledge, community involvement, strategic management, and a dedication to sustainability.

Profit with Purpose

All organizations have a purpose, which is commonly defined as their organizational or corporate mission, or mission statement. It is what guides the direction of operations and decisions top-down; and, in the majority of cases when effectively transmitted, also provides collaborators with a sense of belonging and drive which ultimately impacts their goal achievement and, in turn, those of the organization. In social enterprises, the purpose aspect of profit with purpose refers to an organization's social mission which, therefore, is part of a socially grounded corporate philosophy that includes a socially oriented vision, core values, and social objectives, strategies, and tactics. Much like with other types of organizations, as the social mission is present in organizational decision-making and, therefore, throughout the enterprise's operations, it increases the probability of effective goal achievement; moreover, doing so may enhance effective coordination, which entails both effective collaboration and cooperation, further promoting the organization's social mission.

Profit with purpose is an ideology that certain organizational leaders follow when they are convinced that successful organizational performance ought to be derived from doing good for society, or at least the community that surrounds them. This is accomplished, then, with the objective of balancing their contribution to societal and environmental well-being as well as to the attainment of business growth. For such matter, profit with purpose aligns well with social enterprises and social entrepreneurship; for instance, according to Barrera Duque (2007), social enterprises seek to solve social issues profitably; in other words, executing profit with purpose. They do so by generating both social impact and change (Young, 2006). Moreover, according to Besley and Ghatak (2017), social enterprises are successful because they work to attain profit by achieving their social mission, their purpose.

There are three main aspects that make up the structure of social enterprises, these being: "social missions, revenue streams, and profit distributions" (Hisyam & Lin, 2023, p. 1) which, incidentally, are also a differentiator with other types of firms. Organizations that engage in profit with purpose tend to be more flexible and can find an adequate balance between organizational efficiency, which may yield sufficient profit margins or income to cover costs and remain competitive, and their purpose, i.e., social mission, which drives social and environmental change and well-being. As such, profit with purpose may have a positive effect on both business and social growth and development.

While organizations taking on a profit-with-purpose approach are not motivated by profit (Levillain et al., 2019), the latter is what drives the achievement of the organization's purpose (George et al., 2021), and it is also derived from achieving said purpose. In other words, their overall success is determined by the effects their operations and decisions have on society (Dees & Anderson, 2003), as opposed to solely their bottom line. With this in mind, the specific way in which organizations execute profit with purpose may vary among and within industries and sectors, as well as the organizations themselves. To clarify, the way that each social enterprise manages its approach to profit with purpose will depend on their specific strategic objectives, as well as their strategies and tactics.

Managing Profit with Purpose

Social enterprises are managed just like any other organization. Meaning that their leaders are equally tasked with developing and instilling the organization's corporate philosophy, corporate governance, culture, as well as designing the structure, selecting mechanisms of control, developing strategic plans, and so on and so forth. Further, in terms of management, social enterprises are similar to organizations that are socially responsible or are aligned with a social purpose; in such a way that their leadership tends to be more democratic as well as transformational, their structure tends to the horizontal, network or team-based, and their strategic decision-making is likely to be decentralized encouraging collaborator participation. Organizations that adopt a profit-with-purpose approach to business acknowledge that they have an important role in sustainable development. That said, a common misconception is that social enterprises and social entrepreneurships are socially responsible solely because of the social mission, or because they have adopted a profit-with-purpose approach. Organizations that state to be socially responsible usually actively and proactively engage in corporate social responsibility, which differs from the dual mission of social enterprises.

There are four main ways, or approaches to business dynamics, in which profit with purpose can be managed, that is through the triple-bottom-line (TBL), stakeholder management, engaging in social enterprise responsibility, and sustainable development. While all of these can contribute positively to society and the environment and generate positive financial returns, their characteristics are varied. It goes without saying that all four share two fundamental principles: (1) that growth follows social impact and that supporting the community is carried out by engaging with it, with society; and (2) that ethics, at least at the legal standard, should be at the core of all decisions, policies, and actions. Social enterprises may use the TBL (Elkington, 1997), as previously defined, as an approach to management for the basis of their business model to ensure that they are working toward sustainability driven by their core operations. It may also be used to measure the success of social enterprises; that is, in terms of the 3Ps, people, planet, and profit, and their effect on organizational performance.

Stakeholder management stems from stakeholder theory (Freeman, 1984) and when associated with profit with purpose entails weaving all interested parties' concerns into the organization's decision-making; by doing so, their welfare, growth, and development are an intricate part of its strategic objectives, strategies, and tactics. Social enterprises can move toward a more holistic approach which would entail expanding their business model to one that is also socially responsible. Meaning that it would be aligned with the organization's corporate philosophy, be ethical and sustainable, generate and optimize social, environment, and financial performance, co-create value with stakeholders, and operate for, through, and because of society.

Many organizational leaders are mostly concerned with the effects of their decisions on financial performance; meaning, they either consider social objectives and social responsibility practices an unnecessary cost, as opposed to an investment, or believe that they do not yield a substantial return. However, a McKinsey report found that firms' sustainability programs have a strong positive effect on their financial performance (Bonini & Swartz, 2014). Tansan et al. (2023) have stated that when organizations are not doing their part to be sustainable and propel sustainable practices, they may suffer a negative effect on their competitiveness, both domestically and internationally. Social enterprises, due to their dual mission, already address social and/or environmental objectives. This does not ensure the successful management of their business model; however, a socially responsible approach may positively impact their management for effective attainment of profit with purpose.

Social enterprise responsibility derives from corporate social responsibility, which means that understanding the latter is essential to the former's engagement. In 1949, Dempsey discussed responsible business practices as a means for social justice, to improve society's overall well-being (Dempsey, 1949). Then, two years later, Abrams (1951) posited that organizations' responsibilities should extend to other interested parties, meaning that they should go beyond generating profit for shareholders. Another couple of years later, in 1953, Bowen coined the term corporate social responsibility and argued that managements' decisions should be aligned with society's interests (Bowen, 2013b). Based on these definitions, and particularly Bowen's contribution, the concept of corporate social responsibility has been evolving for over seven decades while being influenced by the various changes and challenges of each decade, as well as technological, innovative, and theoretical advancements.

Although there are numerous definitions for social responsibility, the general consensus says that corporate social responsibility (CSR) is based on three main pillars, these being: social, environmental, and financial performance (Torugsa et al., 2013); that is, in order to be engaged in CSR organizations should design and execute objectives and strategies aimed to achieve a balanced performance of all three. Only focusing on one or two of these elements will not lead to authentic social responsibility. Many confuse social responsibility with philanthropy; while it can be an associated variable, it does not qualify as CSR engagement. For instance, CSR has been defined as including aspects associated with "business ethics, corporate philanthropy, corporate citizenship, sustainability and environmental responsibility" (Matten & Moon, 2007, p. 339); in such a way that corporate social responsibility is an approach to business dynamics which describes how the organization operates internally and externally, by society and for society, to maximize positive effects on society and the environment and achieve competitive advantage through business and social growth and development (López-Fernández, 2015). Even though it continues to largely be a voluntary practice (Godfrey et al., 2009), with the exception of a few countries such as India, Indonesia, and China (Lin, 2020), amongst others, the approach to these laws remains in question; in other words, whether or not they are genuinely focused on CSR achievement or are merely oriented toward philanthropy, social marketing, or disclosure. Furthermore, society's expectations of organizations' ethical, socially responsible behavior are higher than ever.

Corporate social responsibility can be viewed as an umbrella concept; that is an approach to business dynamics that encompasses a series of attributes that go beyond the three main pillars of social development (i.e., social, environmental, and financial performance), including fair commerce, laws and regulations, business plans and intentions, communication and transparency, products and/or services, industrial relations, operations, and work environment. Social responsibility, then, is not only associated with social entrepreneurship, but is also part of their organizational strategy and, therefore, key to their success (Hartzmark & Sussman, 2019).

Social enterprise responsibility (SER) is an approach to social enterprise business dynamics entailing commitment to business and social growth and development with the cooperation and collaboration of its stakeholders. As previously mentioned, these organizations already work toward social and/or environmental objectives and, technically, their dual mission features social and financial intentions, however, they rarely integrate social, environmental, and financial performance in their philosophy and, therefore, within their strategic objectives, strategies, and tactics throughout the enterprise's operations. Further, major areas of opportunity for social entrepreneurs are their mismanagement, particularly financial mismanagement, as well as community responsiveness, which hinder potential partnerships and scalability. Therefore, a social enterprise responsibility approach may assist in fulfilling their mission toward profit with purpose.

The attributes of CSR, therefore, may also be applied to social enterprise responsibility, thereby enabling a holistic approach to the enterprise's dynamics. Figure 2.2 depicts the attributes of CSR which are also applicable to SER. All attributes are interrelated and, for each of them, there are associated stakeholders who should be properly engaged and managed by the organization. Moreover, engaging in social enterprise responsibility also positively impacts sustainable development. The reality is that by addressing the concerns of all stakeholders with the approach to their welfare and growth, the attributes well align with the aims and indicators established to achieve sustainable development globally. In other words, SER encompasses aspects associated with: the triple-bottom-line, stakeholder management, and sustainable development.

Sustainable development (United Nations, 1987), as defined by the United Nations and described in Chapter 1, has significantly informed the way that both corporate social responsibility and social enterprises are approached because it requires considering the well-being of current, potential, and future stakeholders in the organizations' strategic decision-making; in such a way that a social enterprise that manages its profit with purpose via social enterprise responsibility tends to their current, as well as future stakeholders' needs and wants positively impacting the organization and society, through stakeholder engagement. And, in doing so, they are able to positively impact human and sustainable development by reducing poverty and improving social health and housing because social entrepreneurs would not just rely on certain stakeholders' volunteership, but would collaborate with them, creating important partnerships

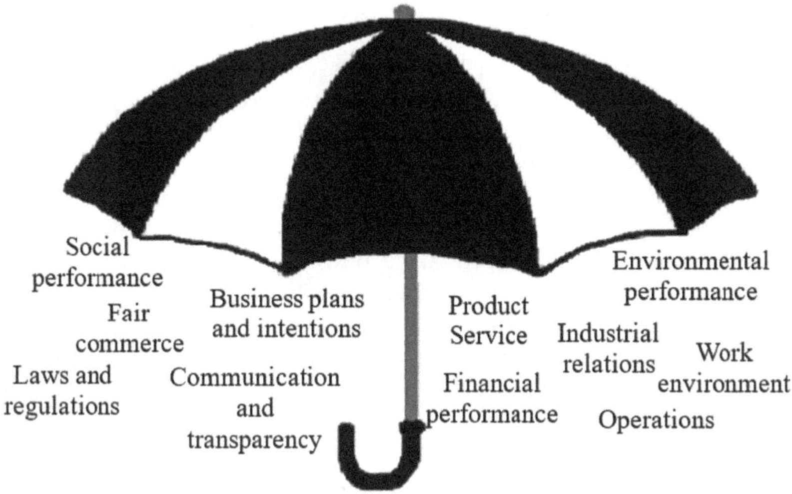

Fig. 2.2 Social responsibility attributes

to ensure that their strategic objectives are met and, ideally, scaling the enterprise through a responsible profit with purpose model.

Social enterprise responsibility and sustainable development, therefore, suggest that organizations' accountability extends the legal standard of ethics toward both business and social growth and development; in other words, it goes beyond the minimum operation conditions indicated by local, national, and sometimes international, regulatory authorities. Stakeholders are increasingly interested in associating with organizations that demonstrate a commitment to social and environmental responsibility, as these practices enable the creation of shared value which aligns business success with societal progress. Moreover, social enterprises that successfully implement profit with purpose more often than not may find that it not only enhances their reputation, as their image is improved, but also contributes to long-term sustainability and resilience.

Social Enterprises' Impact on Social Development

As previously mentioned in Chapter 1, governments, especially those in emerging markets and developing countries, have found it particularly difficult to meet the needs of their populations, let alone meet their expectations; social entrepreneurs have been working toward alleviating at least part of their burden by taking on particular social issues (Davis et al., 2021) that permeate society; in such a way that social enterprises have, in some form or another, been taking on the responsibility of hindering the negative effects on countries' social growth and development. At the very least, the increased number of social enterprises as well as research on the matter, are telling of the fact that there is a particular interest in finding new ways to foster well-being by sharing responsibility (Gaiger et al., 2019) for its achievement.

Social enterprises can develop a social mission that is directly associated with sustainability yet has a collateral positive effect on social welfare. Social enterprises can also forge a social mission that directly aims to reduce poverty, improve social health, as well as increase dignified housing. To be clear, their mission can be specifically aimed at either of the three aspects or can aim to impact all three. Having said that, it is also possible to have a different social mission and still have a positive impact on one or all of said aspects. In other words, even when the main purpose of these organizations is not to, for example, alleviate poverty, the latter can become a significant collateral effect of their operations. In fact, anytime an organization takes on a social approach to business, there are collateral effects on well-being that should be considered in the organization's strategic design as well as performance.

In relation to housing, social enterprises may impact communities in need of affordable housing solutions by promoting the construction of housing units that are targeted to low-income families or individuals. This can be done, for example, either by working in the actual construction or by collaborating with construction organizations. Their operations may also be related to the creation of innovative solutions to promote sustainable housing development which are characterized by a reduced carbon footprint, efficient energy, and/or water use, amongst others. Their social mission may aim to assist people who are unhoused, which can be done by developing shelters or working with shelter providers, as well as creating innovative solutions related to supportive or transitioning housing. When social enterprises undertake any of the above housing issues, they are also able to impact the served communities' overall prosperity which is associated with levels of poverty and as well as their health. The same can occur with social enterprises whose purpose is to alleviate poverty and positively influence social health.

Global Entrepreneurship Monitor (GEM) has reported that Latin America and the Caribbean has become a burgeoning center for entrepreneurship (GEM, 2023). There are many examples of social enterprises in Latin America and the Caribbean with a variety of core businesses and missions. Take, for example, the enterprise *Ejido Verde* which operates in Mexico. They are a social development organization dedicated to the supply of resin-derived products. Their social mission is to "reactivate pine resin production through its innovative reforestation model, to regenerate degraded lands by establishing commercial agroforestry plantations with the purpose of taking advantage of pine resin" (Ejido Verde, 2023). They do so by implementing a business model that enables producers from low-income forest communities to capture the majority of wealth which derives from harvesting and supplying resin products (Ejido Verde, 2023). Another example is the enterprise *Red de alimentos* which operates in Chile. It is a social, private, for-profit, organization which created the first food bank in the country in question. Their social mission is to bring organizations and vulnerable people together by providing them with basic goods. They do so by means of a sustainable business model (Red de alimentos, 2023) based on the triple-bottom-line.

CaribShare, which operates in Jamaica and the Caribbean, is a not-for-profit social enterprise that aims to promote sustainable waste management by creating solutions for food waste and organic waste recycling (CaribShare, 2023). Their model works by retrieving organic waste from various sources, such as hotels and farms, to be converted into biogas and fertilizer; their programs have a direct impact on society and business; these include converting waste into energy to supply businesses that are working toward self-generating energy, converting waste into fertilizer for farmers, and also converting waste into profits for farmers and hotels (Jamaica Conservation Partners, 2023). The founder also develops a blog called Food Waste Blog (CaribShare, 2023) which enables keeping current and potential stakeholders informed of the issues and created solutions. Another example *Sos Nicaragua*, meaning You are Nicaragua, is a social enterprise dedicated to friendly, conservation tourism with a strong commitment with sustainable development; it operates by connecting people with the environment. Their mission is to impact social awareness and commitment toward social and environmental development "through the promotion of solidarity tourism and the active participation of civil society in local projects oriented to social and environmental welfare" (Sos Nicaragua, 2024). They invest half of their revenue in social and environmental programs and their supply chain includes local companies (Sos Nicaragua, 2024), which enhances their business growth and development, as well as that of the organizations' collaborators. Therefore, their operations have a direct and positive effect on social development.

In the above examples, the enterprises work toward social and environmental well-being, and their operations, in turn, positively impact other social issues. For instance, the innovative reforestation model has a positive impact on the environment which can de-escalate extreme weather conditions, reducing the probability of displaced communities. Just from the perspective of the organization's supply chain, by working with producers from low-income forest communities, there is not only a positive effect on the environment by consuming locally, but there is also a positive effect on poverty. The latter may positively impact the communities' health and housing. Then comes the ripple effect, meaning that by creating a positive effect on the social development of the communities with which they collaborate and for whom they operate, there are collateral effects on other interested parties' development as well.

The second example is quite similar; food banks directly and positively impact people that are facing food insecurity and hunger. This improves recipients' nutrition and health. Some food banks are able to collect, store, and distribute food that would otherwise be disposed of, discarded. In doing so, there is a significant reduction in waste, as well as a decrease in pollutants which positively impacts the environment. The implications of the mentioned effects also positively impact the communities' levels of poverty and may lead to a decrease in unemployment which, in turn, can positively impact the communities' housing situation. In the third example, managing waste has a positive impact on society and the environment by impacting poverty, as rural areas' development is strengthened, as well as climate change. And in the fourth example, conservation tourism has a positive impact on sustainable development; society, businesses, and the environment are all benefited as the model works by strengthening the performance of their supply chain through sustainable practices. By doing so, the organizations in the supply chain are significantly benefited, positively impacting their growth and development and, in turn, the development of their families, communities, as well as the environment itself.

Therefore, a single conduit, the social enterprise, through their leaders' vision and actions, can channel resources for not only the organization's purpose, but also to transfer benefits to other interested parties. In a sense, social enterprises that generate profit with purpose may inspire and accelerate business strategies aiming to achieve profit for social development. In fact, in doing so, they take significant steps toward shifting their countries from emerging sustainable development toward sustained development and quality of life. What is missing is the proactive collaboration and cooperation of current and potential stakeholders to create strategic partnerships and be able to scale their business models, in turn, enhancing their scope of impact and influence. Hence, as interested parties are of central importance for the operation and success of social enterprises, their influence will be further analyzed in the following chapter.

References

Abrams, F. W. (1951). Management's responsibilities in a complex world. *Harvard Business Review, XXIX*(3), 29–34.

Aguirre Quezada, J. C., & Flores Muñoz, M. C. (2018). El emprendimiento en Latinoamérica. Un impacto diferenciable para el crecimiento económico entre países de la región. *Revista Espacios*, 39(32). Retrieved March 27th, 2024 from https://www.revistaespacios.com/a18v39n32/a18v39n32p02.pdf

Anheier, H. K. (2001). Voluntary Associations, Sociology of. In N. J. Smelser, & P. B. Baltes, (Eds.) *International Encyclopedia of the Social & Behavioral Sciences* (pp. 16302–16306). https://doi.org/10.1016/B0-08-043076-7/02009-X

Austin, J. E. (2006). Three avenues for social entrepreneurship research. In J. Mair, J. Robinson, & K. Hockerts (Eds.), *Social entrepreneurship* (pp. 22–33). Palgrave Macmillan.

Austin, J., Stevenson, H., & Wei-Skillern, J. (2006). Social and commercial entrepreneurship: Same, different, or both? *Entrepreneurship Theory & Practice, 30*(1), 1–22. https://doi.org/10.1111/j.1540-6520.2006.00107

Barrera Duque, E. (2007). La empresa social y su responsabilidad social. *INNOVAR. Revista de Ciencias Administrativas y Sociales*. 17(30), 59–75. https://www.redalyc.org/pdf/818/81803006.pdf

Bass, B.M. (1990). *Bass & Stogdill's handbook of leadership. Theory, research, & managerial implications*. The Free Press.

Besley, T., & Ghatak, M. (2017). Profit with purpose? A theory of social enterprise. *American Economic Journal: Economic Policy, 9*(3), 19–58. https://doi.org/10.1257/pol.20150495

Bonini, S., & Swartz, S. (2014). *Profits with purpose: How organizing for sustainability can benefit the bottom line* (pp. 5–15). McKinsey & Company. Retrieved March 29th, 2023 from: https://www.mckinsey.de/~/media/mckinsey/industries/consumer%20packaged%20goods/our%20insights/getting%20the%20most%20out%20of%20your%20sustainability%20program/srp_2014_profits%20with%20purpose.pdf

Bonnici, F., Klijn, V., Nowack, D., Bennett, T., & Gregory, D. (2024). *The State of Social Enterprise: A Review of Global Data 2013–2023. Insight Report*. SCHWAB Foundation & The World Economic Forum. Retrieved May 8th, 2024, from: https://www3.weforum.org/docs/WEF_The_State_of_Social_Enterprise_2024.pdf

Boons, F., & Wagner, M. (2009). Assessing the relationship between economic and ecological performance: Distinguishing system levels and the role of innovation. *Ecological Economics, 68*(7), 1908–1914. https://doi.org/10.1016/j.ecolecon.2009.02.012

Borzaga, C., Galera, G., Franchini, B., Chiomento, S., Nogales, R., & Carini, C. (2020). *Social enterprises and their ecosystems in Europe: Comparative synthesis report*. European Commission. https://base.socioeco.org/docs/social_enterprises_and_their_ecosystems_in_europe._comparative_synthesis_report.pdf

Bowen, G. A. (2013a). Caribbean civil society: Development role and policy implications. *Nonprofit Policy Forum, 4*(1), 81–97. https://doi.org/10.1515/npf-2012-0013

Bowen, H. R. (2013b). *Social responsibilities of the businessman*. University of Iowa Press.

British Council. (2022). *More in common. The global state of social enterprise*. Retrieved July 4th, 2023 from: https://www.britishcouncil.org/sites/default/files/more_in_common_global_state_of_social_enterprise.pdf

Brown, M. E., & Treviño, L. K. (2006). Ethical leadership: A review and future directions. *The Leadership Quarterly, 17*(6), 595–616. https://doi.org/10.1016/j.leaqua.2006.10.004

Brown, M. E., Treviño, L. K., & Harrison, D. A. (2005). Ethical leadership: A social learning perspective for construct development and testing. *Organizational Behavior and Human Decision Processes, 97*(2), 117–134. https://doi.org/10.1016/j.obhdp.2005.03.002

CaribShare. (2023). *About CaribShare*. Retrieved August 2nd, 2023, from: https://www.caribshareja.com/

CEPAL. (2023). *Micro, small and medium-sized enterprises (MSMEs)*. United Nations. Retrieved November 12th, 2023 from: https://www.cepal.org/en/subtopics/micro-small-and-medium-sized-enterprises-msmes

Condes, Y. (2021). *A centuries-old legacy of mutual aid lives on in Mexican American communities*. PBS of Southern California. Retrieved October 7th, 2023, from: https://www.pbssocal.org/shows/lost-la/a-centuries-old-legacy-of-mutual-aid-lives-on-in-mexican-american-communities

Corry, O. (2010). Defining and theorizing the third sector. In R. Taylor (Ed.), *Third sector research* (pp. 11–20). Springer.

Davis, P. E., Bendickson, J. S., Muldoon, J., & McDowell, W. C. (2021). Agency theory utility and social entrepreneurship: Issues of identity and role conflict. *Review of Managerial Science, 15*, 2299–2318. https://doi.org/10.1007/s11846-020-00423-y

De Beule, F., Bruneel, J., & Dobson, K. (2023). The internationalization of social enterprises: The impact of business model characteristics. *International Business Review, 32*(6), 102188. https://doi.org/10.1016/j.ibusrev.2023.102188

Dees, J. G. (1998). *The meaning of "Social Entrepreneurship". The Kauffman Center for Entrepreneurial Leadership*. Retrieved March 20th, 2024 from: https://centers.fuqua.duke.edu/case/wp-content/uploads/sites/7/2015/03/Article_Dees_MeaningofSocialEntrepreneurship_2001.pdf

Dees, J. G., & Anderson, B. B. (2003). For-profit social ventures. In M. L. Kourilsky & W. B. Walstad (Eds.), *Social entrepreneurship* (pp. 1–26). Senate Hall Academic Publishing.

Dees, J. G., & Anderson, B. B. (2006). Framing a theory of social entrepreneurship: Building on two schools of practice and thought. In R. Mosher-Williams, (Ed.). *Research on social entrepreneurship: Understanding and contributing to an emerging field*, (pp. 39–66). Association for Research on Nonprofit Organizations and Voluntary Action (ARNOVA).

Defourny, J., & Nyssens, M. (2010). Social enterprise. In K. Hart, J.-L. Laville, & A. D. Cattani (Eds.), *The human economy: A citizen's guide* (pp. 284–292). Polity Press.

Del Cerro, J. (2016). *¿Qué es el emprendimiento social? Negocios que cambian el mundo*. NEISA (Nueva Editorial Iztaccihuatl).

Dempsey, B. W. (1949). The roots of business responsibility. *Harvard Business Review, 27*, 393–404.

Doherty, B., Haugh, H., & Lyon, F. (2014). Social enterprises as hybrid organizations: A review and research agenda. *International Journal of Management Reviews, 16*(4), 417–436. https://doi.org/10.1111/ijmr.12028

Dueñas, A. E. P., & Cedeño, S. M. R. (2020). El emprendimiento en América Latina: Un análisis de su etimología, tipología y proceso. *ECA Sinergia, 11*(2), 47–58. https://doi.org/10.33936/eca_sinergia.v11i2.2115

During, R. (2016). *Evolutionary theory of social enterprise. On the use of evolutionary concepts in the field of social entrepreneurship*. EFESEIIS. (pp. 1–21). Retrieved January 20th, 2023, from: https://edepot.wur.nl/428150

Ejido Verde. (2023). *Nuestro modelo*. Retrieved August 3rd, 2023, from: https://ejidoverde.com/es/

El Ebrashi, R. (2013). Social entrepreneurship theory and sustainable social impact. *Social Responsibility Journal, 9*(2), 188–209. https://doi.org/10.1108/SRJ-07-2011-0013

Elkington, J. (1997). *Cannibals with Forks: The Triple Bottom Line of 21st Century Business*. Capstone.

Fowler, A. (2000). NGDOs as a moment in history: Beyond aid to social entrepreneurship or civic innovation? *Third World Quarterly., 21*(4), 637–654. https://doi.org/10.1080/713701063

Freeman, R. E. (1984). *Strategic management: A stakeholder approach*. Pitman.

Gaiger, L. I., Nyssens, M., & Wanderley, F. (2019). *Social enterprise in Latin America, Theory*. Routledge.

García, M. L. S., Adame, M. E. C., & Saenz, M. E. V. (2020). Una aproximación a los conceptos de emprendedor y emprendimiento social. *Universidad & Empresa, 22*(39), 1–27.

GEM. (2023). *Global Entrepreneurship Monitor 2023/2024 Global Report: 25 Years and Growing*. GEM.

George, G., Haas, M. R., McGahan, A. M., Schillebeeckx, S. J. D., & Tracey, P. (2021). Purpose in the for-profit firm: A review and framework for management research. *Journal of Management*. https://doi.org/10.1177/01492063211006450

Godfrey, P. C., Merrill, C. B., & Hansen, J. M. (2009). The relationship between corporate social responsibility and shareholder value: An empirical test of the risk management hypothesis. *Strategic Management Review, 30*(4), 425–445. https://doi.org/10.1002/smj.750

Gupta, V. K., & Bhawe, N. M. (2007). The influence of proactive personality and stereotype threat on women's entrepreneurial intentions. *Journal of Leadership and Organizational Studies., 13*(4), 73–85. https://doi.org/10.1177/10717919070130040901

Halsall, J. P., Snowden, M., Clegg, P., Mswaka, W., Alderson, M., Hyams-Ssekasi, D., Oberoi, R., & Winful, E. C. (2022). Social enterprise as a model for change: Mapping a global cross-disciplinary framework. *Entrepreneurship Education, 5*, 425–446. https://doi.org/10.1007/s41959-022-00084-w

Hartzmark, S. M. & Sussman, A. B. (2019) Do investors value sustainability? A natural experiment examining ranking and fund flows. Finance Working Paper No. 565/2018. *European Corporate Governance Institute (ECGI)* (pp. 1–60). Retrieved March 25th, 2023 from: http://ssrn.com/abstract_id=3016092

Heinecke, A., Kloibhofer, M., & Krzeminska, A. (2014). *Leadership in social enterprise how to manage yourself and the team*. The World Economic Forum. Retrieved September 11th, 2023, from: https://www3.weforum.org/docs/WEF_leadership_in_social_enterprise_2014.pdf

Hisyam & Lin, S-W. (2023). Bibliometric analysis of social enterprise literature: Revisit to regroup. *Journal of Innovation & Knowledge, 8*(3), 1–14 https://doi.org/10.1016/j.jik.2023.100411

Improvement and Development Agency. (2008). *FOSS. Working with the third sector*. Retrieved June 2nd, 2023 from: https://www.local.gov.uk/sites/default/files/documents/working-third-sector-pdf--1ab.pdf

International Cooperative Alliance. (2018). *The Rochdale Pioneers*. Our History. Retrieved October 8th, 2023, from: https://www.ica.coop/en/cooperatives/history-cooperative-movement#:~:text=The%20earliest%20record%20of%20a,forming%20the%20Fenwick%20Weavers'%20Society

Jamaica Conservation Partners. (2023). *CaribSahre Biogas*. Retrieved August 2nd, 2023 from: https://www.jamaicaconservationpartners.org/caribshare-biogas/

Koryak, O., Mole, K. F., Lockett, A., Hayton, J. C., Ucbasaran, D., & Hodgkinson, G. P. (2015). Entrepreneurial leadership, capabilities and firm growth. *International Small Business Journal: Researching Entrepreneurship., 33*(1), 89–105. https://doi.org/10.1177/0266242614558315

Kramer, M. R., & Pfitzer, M. W. (2016). *The ecosystem of shared value*. Harvard Business Review. Business and Society. Retrieved September 1st, 2023, from: https://hbr.org/2016/10/the-ecosystem-of-shared-value

Landström, H. (1999). The roots of entrepreneurial research. *New England Journal of Entrepreneurship, 2*(2), 9–20.

Leadbeater, C. (1997). *The rise of the social entrepreneur*. London: DEMOS. Retrieved April 2nd, 2023 from: https://demos.co.uk/wp-content/uploads/2023/03/theriseofthesocialentrepreneur.pdf

Lederman, D., Messina, J., Pienknagura, S., & Rigolini, J. (2014). *El emprendimiento en América Latina. Muchas empresas y poca innovación*. Banco Internacional de Reconstrucción y Fomento/ Banco Mundial. Retrieved April 3rd, 2024, from: https://www.worldbank.org/content/dam/Worldbank/document/LAC/EmprendimientoAmericaLatina_resumen.pdf

Lepoutre, J., Justo, R., Terjesen, S., & Bosma, N. (2013). Designing a global standardized methodology for measuring social entrepreneurship activity: The global entrepreneurship monitor social entrepreneurship study. *Small Business Economics, 40*, 693–714. https://doi.org/10.1007/s11187-011-9398-4

Levillain, K., Segrestin, B., & Hatchuel, A. (2019). Profit-with-purpose corporations: An innovation in corporate law to meet contemporary CSR challenges. In A. McWilliams, D. E. Rupp, D. S. Siegel, G. K. Stahl, & D. A. Waldman, (Eds.). *The Oxford handbook of corporate social responsibility: Psychological and organizational perspectives* (pp. 490–513). https://doi.org/10.1093/oxfordhb/9780198802280.013.21

Levy, D.C. (1996). *Building the Third Sector: Latin America's Private Research Centers and nonprofit development*. University of Pittsburgh Press.

Light, P. C. (2009). Social entrepreneurship revisited. *Stanford Social Innovation Review, 7*(3), 21–22. https://doi.org/10.48558/Z8K2-W870

Lin, L.-W. (2020). Mandatory corporate social responsibility? Legislative innovation and judicial application in China. *The American Journal of Comparative Law, 68*(3), 576–615. https://doi.org/10.1093/ajcl/avaa025

López-Fernández, A. M. (2015). *Convergence of corporate social responsibility and business growth: Collateral effects on business and society*. NOVA Publishers.

Luke, B., & Chu, V. (2013). Social enterprise versus social entrepreneurship: An examination of the 'why' and 'how' in pursuing social change. *International Small Business Journal: Researching Entrepreneurship, 31*(7), 764–784. https://doi.org/10.1177/0266242612462598

MacDonald, M., & Howorth, C. (2018). Roots of social enterprise: Entrepreneurial philanthropy, England 1600–1908. *Social Enterprise Journal, 14*(1), 4–21. https://doi.org/10.1108/SEJ-03-2017-0020

Mair, J., & Martí, I. (2006). Social entrepreneurship research: A source of explanation, prediction, and delight. *Journal of World Business, 41*(1), 36–44. https://doi.org/10.1016/j.jwb.2005.09.002

Mair, J., & Noboa, E. (2006). Social entrepreneurship: How intentions to create a social venture are formed. In J. Mair, J. Robinson, & K. Hockerts (Eds.), *Social entrepreneurship* (pp. 121–135). Palgrave Macmillan.

Matten, D., & Moon, J. (2007). Pan-European approach. A conceptual framework for understanding CSR. In W. C. Zimmerli, M. Holzinger, & K. Richter (Eds.), *Corporate ethics and corporate governance*. Springer.

Monguí Pintenel, J. (2023). Contexto del emprendimiento social. En una mirada al emprendimiento social en Colombia (pp. 16–39). *Corporación Universitaria Minuto de Dios. UNIMINUTO*. https://doi.org/10.26620/uniminuto/978-958-763-620-8.cap.1

Northern Bridge. (2023). *What is the third sector and what does it do?* Northern Bridge Doctoral Training Partnership. Retrieved June 2nd, 2023, from: http://toolkit.northernbridge.ac.uk/engagingwithpolicymakers/engagingwiththethirdsector/whatisthethirdsectorandwhatdoesitdo/

Noya, A. (2014). *Social enterprises: What can policies do to support them?* United Nations Economic Commission for Europe (UNECE). KBD Newsletter. Retrieved August 7th, 2023, from: https://unece.org/fileadmin/DAM/ceci/documents/KBD_Newsletter/Issue_4/Noya_OECD.pdfx

OECD. (1999). *Social enterprises*. OECD Publishing.

Osorio-Novela, G., Mungaray-Lagarda, A., & Ramírez-Angulo, N. (2021). Social Enterprise in Mexico, a new business classification. *Sustainability, 13*(16), 9264. https://doi.org/10.3390/su13169264

Portales, L., & Pérez, O. A. (2015). Emprendimiento y Empresa Social Como Estrategia De Desarrollo Local. *Dans Recherches en Sciences de Gestion, 6*(111), 137–160. https://doi.org/10.3917/resg.111.0137

Prado, A. (2021). *Emprendimiento Social en América Latina: Buenas prácticas para llevar productos y servicios a poblaciones rurales de escasos recursos*. INCAE Business School. Retrieved March 29th, 2023, from: https://cnnespanol.cnn.com/wp-content/uploads/2021/06/Reporte-Emprendimiento-Social-en-Ame%CC%81rica-Latina_Andrea-Prado-INCAE_VF.pdf

Preghenella, N., & Battistella, C. (2021). Exploring business models for sustainability: A bibliographic investigation of the literature and future research directions. *Business Strategy and the Environment, 30*(5), 2505–2522. https://doi.org/10.1002/bse.2760

Red de alimentos. (2023). *Qué hacemos*. Retrieved August 3rd, 2023, from: https://www.redalimentos.cl/que-hacemos-que-nada-sobre/

Robinson, J. (2006). Navigating social and institutional barriers to markets: How social entrepreneurs identify and evaluate opportunities. In J. Mair, J. Robinson, & K. Hockerts (Eds.), *Social entrepreneurship* (pp. 95–120). Palgrave Macmillan.

Rufer, L. S., Rufer, R. J., & Hanspal, S. (2021). Micro organization use of social media for business-to-business customers. In M. Khosrow-Pour (Ed.), *Encyclopedia of organizational knowledge administration and technology* (pp. 2140–2152). IGI Global.

Santos, F. M. (2012). A positive theory of social entrepreneurship. *Journal of Business Ethics, 111*(3), 335–351. https://doi.org/10.1007/s10551-012-1413-4

Schumpeter, J. A. (1934). *The theory of economic development*. Harvard University Press.

Shaw, E., & Carter, S. (2007). Social entrepreneurship: Theoretical antecedents and empirical analysis of entrepreneurial processes and outcomes. *Journal of Small Business and Enterprise Development, 14*(3), 418–434. https://doi.org/10.1108/14626000710773529

Short, C. J., Moss, W. T., & Lumpkin, G. T. (2009). Research in social entrepreneurship: Past contributions and future opportunities. *Strategic Entrepreneurship Journal, 3*(2), 161–194. https://doi.org/10.1002/sej.69

Singh, B., Narain, R., & Yadav, R. C. (2012). Identifying critical barriers in the growth of Indian micro, small and medium enterprises (MSMEs). *International Journal of Business Competition and Growth, 2*(1), 84–105. https://doi.org/10.1504/IJBCG.2012.044057

Sos Nicaragua. (2024). *Our model*. Retrieved May 1st, 2024, from: https://sosnicaragua.org/our-model/

Steinerowski, A. A., & Steinerowska-Streb, I. (2012). Can social enterprise contribute to creating sustainable rural communities? Using the lens of structuration theory to analyse the emergence of rural social enterprise. *Local Economy: The Journal of the Local Economy Policy Unit, 27*(2), 167–182. https://doi.org/10.1177/0269094211429650

Tansan, B., Lang, N., Meyer, M., Gökbulut, A., Ivers,L., Hutchinson, R., Santamarta, S., Azevedo, D., & Chan, T. (2023) . *The sustainability imperative in emerging markets*. Retrieved September 16th, 2023 from BCG: https://www.bcg.com/publications/2023/the-importance-of-sustainability-in-business

Teece, D. J. (2010). Business models, business strategy and innovation. *Long Range Planning, 43*(2–3), 172–194. https://doi.org/10.1016/j.lrp.2009.07.003

Thompson, A. (2001). ¿Del compromiso a la eficiencia? Los rumbos del Tercer Sector en América Latina. *Colección*. Número Extraordinario 1, 47–54. Retrieved April 30th, 2024, from: https://repositorio.uca.edu.ar/bitstream/123456789/10088/1/compromiso-eficiencia-rumbos-tercer.pdf

Torugsa, N. A., O'Donohue, W., & Hecker, R. (2013). Proactive CSR: An empirical analysis of the role of its economic, social and environmental dimensions on the association between capabilities and performance. *Journal of Business Ethics, 115*(2), 383–402. https://doi.org/10.1007/s10551-012-1405-4

Tran, A. T. P., & Von Korflesch, H. (2016). A conceptual model of social entrepreneurial intention based on the social cognitive career theory. *Asia Pacific Journal of Innovation and Entrepreneurship, 10*(1), 17–38. https://doi.org/10.1108/APJIE-12-2016-007

United Nations. (1987). *Report of the World Commission on Environment and Development*. United Nations Digital Library. Retrieved May 9th, 2023, from: https://digitallibrary.un.org/record/139811?ln=en

Vandenberg, P. (2009). *Micro, Small and Medium-Sized Enterprises and the Global Economic Crisis. Impacts and Policy Responses*. International Labour Organization (ILO). Retrieved November 10th, 2023, from: https://www.ilo.org/wcmsp5/groups/public/---ed_emp/---emp_ent/documents/publication/wcms_108413.pdf

Vasconcelos, T. B., de Oliveira, V. M., & Correia, S. E. N. (2022). Indicators of the behavior of social entrepreneurs at the individual level. *Contextus—Revista Contemporânea de Economia e Gestão, 20*, 168–181. https://doi.org/10.19094/contextus.2022.78394

Vidovic, D. (2023). The meaning of being a social entrepreneur in the society of multiple transitions. *Social Enterprise Journal, 19*(3), 237–255. https://doi.org/10.1108/SEJ-08-2022-0075

Young, R. (2006). For what it is worth: social value and the future of social entrepreneurship. In A. Nicholls (Ed.), *Social entrepreneurship: New models of sustainable social change*. Oxford University Press.

Yunus, M. (2010). *Building Social Business: The new kind of capitalism that serves humanity's most pressing needs*. PublicAffairs.

Zhu, Y., Sun, L.-Y., & Leung, A. S. M. (2014). Corporate social responsibility, firm reputation, and firm performance: The role of ethical leadership. *Asia Pacific Journal of Management, 31*(4), 925–947. https://doi.org/10.1007/s10490-013-9369-1

CHAPTER 3

Collaborative Change and the Social Enterprise

Abstract The success of any organization, including social enterprises, is largely determined by the effectiveness of their relationship with their stakeholders. They are elemental to the creation of value and added value, innovativeness, and the achievement of the organization's corporate philosophy, productivity, desired performance, and competitiveness. Importantly, their collective behavior is certainly an inspiration for social enterprise's missions. Thus, effective stakeholder management is key not only to achieving strategic goals, but also business and social growth and development.

Keywords Stakeholders · Activism · Collective behavior · Crowd behavior · Social movements · Collaborative change · Stakeholder network

There has been an ongoing debate for decades on organizations' true responsibilities; in other words, who they should be serving, i.e., the organization itself and its shareholders or other interested parties, and what is the most strategic way of doing so. In the discussion of organizations' responsibility toward society, there are two main schools of thought, these

A. M. López-Fernández, *Co-Creation in Social Enterprises*, Palgrave Studies of Entrepreneurship and Social Challenges in Developing Economies, https://doi.org/10.1007/978-3-031-83449-3_3

being: shareholder theory and stakeholder theory. That is, whether organizations' responsibility ends with the creation of wealth for shareholders, or if their responsibility extends to all their stakeholders. The third group of people in action in social enterprises, all of the organization's interested parties, that is, stakeholders, are analyzed in this chapter. Therefore, this chapter begins with a discussion of shareholder theory and stakeholder theory, as well as stakeholders' roles and intentions within social enterprises. Then, stakeholder networks are proposed, and their effective management is discussed for the achievement of desired performance; then, the different perspectives of stakeholders' actions toward social development are presented and, finally, collective behavior and crowd behavior are described to discuss social movements and social enterprises.

Stakeholder Theory in Social Enterprises

The third group of people in action in social enterprises are the latter's interested parties or their stakeholders. For decades, the central principle of business responsibility was the creation of shareholder wealth. Shareholder theory, developed by Milton Friedman in 1970 (Friedman, 2007) was, then, the name of the game. Based on its characteristics, i.e., using resources to increase the firm's profits ethically (Friedman, 1962), achieving its main goal would seemingly mean that the outcome for or effects on any other interested parties were of no concern to the organization; meaning that aligning with shareholder theory impedes the consideration of other aspects, particularly social concerns. Stakeholder theory was conceived over a decade later, by R. Edward Freeman (1984), thereby providing an alternative for organizational design and decision-making.

Scholars and practitioners swiftly set off a debate, still ongoing, on whether best business practices were aligned with either shareholder theory or stakeholder theory. In other words, what is the organization's true responsibility? Are they, in a sense, solely obligated to pursue benefits for the firm and its shareholders above any other, or should their responsibility extend to all stakeholders. Since then, stakeholder theory has been a particularly significant disruptor in organizations' approach to business because it entails viewing their responsibility on a larger spectrum or seeing the bigger picture. To begin, it requires acknowledging that organizations have stakeholders, then assessing their degree of responsibility, recognizing that the creation of value for the organization is derived from creating value for their stakeholders and, finally, it requires constant business-reflection.

The term stakeholder was coined in 1963 and was understood as the groups that are needed by the organization in order to continue to exist (Freeman & Reed, 1983); in such a way that they would include a diverse group of individuals, organizations, and institutions, whose work is directly or indirectly associated with the effective performance of the organization. Stakeholder theory posits that, in order to achieve organizational success, all of the organization's stakeholders' needs and wants ought to be considered and taken into consideration in its decision-making process, as opposed to merely focusing on shareholders or stockholders' satisfaction. According to Freeman (1984), stakeholders include all interested parties that can affect and/or are affected by an organization's operations and decisions in the pursuit of their goals; in other words, they have a direct or indirect impact on an organization's failure or success (Freeman et al., 2010). There are many scholars and researchers that have built on Freeman's definition of stakeholders. For instance, they have been defined as those who may influence the organization and are interested in its actions (Savage et al., 1991), those who, with legitimate claim on the organization, supply needed resources for successful operations and expect their interests to be promptly satisfied (Hill & Jones, 1992), those who hold a certain degree of legal and/or moral claim on the organization (Langtry, 1994), as well as the interested parties who are influential in the creation of business value (Phillips et al., 2003).

Stakeholders are those that have particular stake, which is deemed as an interest, claim (Weiss, 2014), or concern, that individuals, organizations, and/or institutions may have regarding the organization's policies, actions, as well as its results and performance. For such matter, it is understandable that the types, classification, or groups of stakeholders have been different throughout the years as well as in relation to businesses and market dynamics. Table 3.1 includes a brief description of the groups or classification of stakeholders. In the early 60s, stakeholders were considered shareowners, employees, customers, suppliers, lenders, and society (Freeman & Reed, 1983). However, as the theory's analysis has evolved, so too have the defined stakeholders; it is also true that interested parties can vary depending on the organizations' or researchers' lens of analysis.

Because stakeholder theory considers all interested parties, it is arguably one of the first integral approaches to business dynamics. Even though some organizational leaders may focus on certain stakeholders, or

Table 3.1 Brief description of stakeholder groups

Author(s)	*Stakeholders*
Greenley and Foxall (1996)	Consumers, competitors, employees, shareholders, and unions
Carroll (2004)	Consumers, employees, owners, the community, government, competitors, and the natural environment
Eesley and Lenox (2006)	Customers, employees, suppliers, shareholders, regulators, communities, and mass and social media
Gaur (2013)	Primary stakeholders, usually internal: stockholders, customers, suppliers, creditors, and employees; secondary stakeholders, usually external: general public, communities, activist groups, business support groups and the media
Fernández and Rajagopal (2014)	Shareholders, collaborators, investors, suppliers, clients, regulatory authorities, the community, environment, and the firm
Thornock (2016)	Customers, employees, suppliers, regulators, critics, and competitors
Buchholz et al., (2020)	Shareholders, employees, customers, end users of the company's products or services, suppliers, business partners, the environment, and future generations, as well as broader society
Chithambo et al., (2022)	Shareholders, investors, community, government regulators, employees, customers, suppliers, competitors, NGOs, and media

prioritize a few of them, the theory clearly posits that the success of the organization relies on the inclusion of all interested parties. Proponents of stakeholder theory build on the premise that while profit is important, it is not or should not be the sole purpose of the organization or even the strategic goal on which all other organizational goals are anchored. Of course, contingency theory may be argued in that *it all depends*, precisely in relation to the attributes of the organization's mission. This is why there are still organizational leaders today that committedly endorse and practice shareholder theory. That being said, if an organization aims to encourage both business and social growth and development, thus generate profit with purpose and drive social performance, then, its organizational leaders ought to align their policies, practices, and operations with stakeholder theory. In other words, successful social enterprises well align with stakeholder theory.

Social enterprises have the potential to create value for society through social innovation because of its positive impact on stakeholders (Sekliuckiene & Kisielius, 2015). Social enterprises' stakeholders are no different than those of any other type of organization; meaning that, they are also interested parties that affect and are affected by the enterprise's operations and decisions. According to Donaldson and Preston (1995), stakeholders may be identified as those that have interests in the organization which are considered fundamentally valuable; therefore, the process of identifying stakeholders is the same regardless of the type and/or size of organizations. Having said that, the way they are referred to may vary, particularly in the degree to which they are specified as opposed to a generalized term. However, the need to prioritize their effective management has the same degree of importance. Table 3.2 includes a brief description of stakeholders in social enterprises. The active participation of all stakeholders is reflected in the achievement of the organization's corporate philosophy, in the case of social enterprises, their entrepreneurial or enterprise philosophy.

The inclusion of the environment as one of the enterprises' stakeholders has definitely created an energetic debate among scholars and practitioners. Some have posited that considering the environment as a stakeholder is unfitting (see Orts & Strudler, 2002; Phillips & Reichart, 2000); on the one hand, it has been considered that there are moral implications related to the determination of stakeholders in that there is no need for the organization to have a moral consideration for the environment; it has also been argued that the environment should not be considered a stakeholder because it does not have a relationship with the organization based on financial transactions, and that it does not have a mind and, therefore, cannot demand action from the enterprise. In other words, the arguments are based on the fact that the environment is not human.

On the other hand, it has also been argued that the environment, in fact, has rights (Nash, 1990), therefore, organizations should consider it in their decision-making. According to Starik (1995), organizations have a moral obligation to respect the environment and its resources because it is an economic entity. The fact of the matter is that the environment, just like organizations, is a non-human entity with a stake in the organization. Meaning that, the environment affects and is affected by the organization's operations and decisions; social enterprises should, then, advocate for the environment. Therefore, it is considered that social enterprises,

Table 3.2 A brief description of potential stakeholders in social enterprises

Stakeholders	
Collaborators	All internal parties working toward the achievement of the enterprise's philosophy, regardless of their position or echelon
Beneficiaries	Individuals or groups in a community to whom the enterprise's mission and operations are targeted (sometimes also referred to as the community served)
Consumers	Individuals, institutions, or organizations that purchase services and/or products from the enterprise. They can be part of the community served or beneficiaries
Suppliers	Individuals, institutions, or organizations that provide raw material, services, and/or products for the enterprise's operations
Creditors	Individuals, institutions, or organizations that are owed by the enterprise; the enterprise is in debt with them
Investors	Individuals, institutions, or organizations that provide capital with the expectation of a financial return from the enterprise
Competitors	Institutions or organizations that are direct or indirect contenders of the enterprise in the achievement of profit, consumer attraction and retention, market share, and competitiveness
Regulatory authorities	Government agencies, local, national, and international laws, and international standards that develop and/or control public policies, norms, and laws that limit and regulate the enterprise's operations and practices
Community	Organizations such as NGOs, public organizations, public–private partnerships, opinion formers, social activists, environmentalists, as well as virtual communities; they, at least, surround the enterprise, but tend to extend to the enterprise's span of operations. Virtual communities, however, may be global. It is sometimes associated with beneficiaries when they are directly benefited by the enterprise's operations
Environment	Assortment of natural resources that are consumed and potentially exploited by the enterprise for its operation; they may be directly sourced by the enterprise, or indirectly consumed (i.e., through the enterprise's supply chain)
Volunteers	Individuals or groups that provide services, usually temporarily or sporadically, without remuneration and who contribute to the enterprise's operations and goal achievement
Partners	Associate organizations or enterprises that collaborate with the social enterprise toward the creation of an alliance or joint venture to achieve specific goals

like other organizations, have as much obligation to the environment's well-being as that of their consumers, the community, and shareholders, among other widely acknowledged stakeholders. For social enterprises, the inclusion of the environment is less than a debate and more of a given since their missions are grounded in social development which cannot be achieved without a sustainable approach because social and sustainable development are interconnected.

Stakeholder Engagement

Social enterprise leaders cannot succeed on their own (Light, 2009); they need the participation of the third group of people in action to fulfill their social mission. Stakeholder engagement in social enterprises is elemental to the achievement of strategic plans for desired successful outcomes, and enterprise philosophy attainment. According to Ramus and Vaccaro (2017), internal and external stakeholder engagement is fundamental to achieve an optimal balance between the enterprise's financial and social value objectives; in other words, to remain operational, competitive, and sustain growth and development. Effective engagement requires identifying key stakeholders, including interested parties in strategic goal achievement, actively listening to them, their concerns, needs, and wants, as well as promptly responding to them. Doing so influences the social enterprise's legitimacy, ability to operate and create value for stakeholders and, therefore, the organization.

The stakeholders mentioned in Table 3.2 are stated in their generic form, meaning that there are potentially as many classifications, types, and names of stakeholders as there are organizations. That is, each organization will have certain stakeholders and, furthermore, each organizational project may have additional or less stakeholders on their lists, as some may be selective so as to prioritize by importance or relevance toward goal achievement. As such, identifying stakeholders is an essential task with strong implications on decision-making and, ultimately, the achievement of strategic objectives. There are some common mistakes that organizational leaders and managers make when determining who their stakeholders are. First, some posit that there are, in fact, legitimate stakeholders which would be those that the organization has selected as the individuals and/or organizations that actually matter when it comes to decision-making. This selection is biased as it is based on a preconceived notion that *real stakeholders* are those that have some sort of proof that they are able to improve the organization's condition by producing profit, increasing market share and competitiveness. Second, some also state that for individuals and/or organizations to be stakeholders they should have some sort of claim over the organization accompanied by certain demands. If organizations are truly considering all interested parties, they ought to include current and potential stakeholders; this means everyone. And third, some believe that legitimate stakeholders are those that have calculable peremptory power over an organization's decision-making. All current and potential stakeholders have a certain degree of power over an organization's decision-making, it may not be evident to the organization or even to the stakeholders but, sure enough, it is there. There is, however, a clear-cut way to avoid such mistakes; the key is to not underestimate the influence, impact, and power of any and all current and potential stakeholders. They, indeed, hold the power to make or break a full-blown strategic plan and, therefore, are all essential to the achievement of social enterprises' dual mission.

Social entrepreneurs can create value for their stakeholders in the same way that they are able to engage in social enterprise responsibility, that is, as effectively as any other type of organization, even large and multinational organizations, and despite the organization's core business. According to Smith and Woods (2015), legitimacy may be achieved when social enterprises create value for their stakeholders which, in turn, leads to their stakeholders' support of the organization. It is true that all organizations need their stakeholders in order to operate effectively, however, social enterprises need both stakeholders' participation and support to achieve their goals and execute strategies and tactics. In other words, their support is needed to ensure that they are successfully responding to the related cues in society, or in the community they operate with and for.

As stakeholders can influence the organization's operations and decisions (Savage et al., 1991), actively listening to their concerns and addressing them is particularly relevant for effective stakeholder management. The reality is that considering all stakeholders requires a multilevel reflection, insomuch as organizational leaders should assess whether or not their actions are resonating positively with their stakeholders. For instance, the social entrepreneur should raise the following questions: Have we considered what our stakeholders need and/or want? Are we aware of how our stakeholders have responded to our actions and results? Are our stakeholders' responses being considered in our current and future decision-making? And are organizational decisionmakers measuring the effects of stakeholder participation in the organization's growth and development? In other words, are the enterprise's stakeholders' voices being heard? Do they have an ongoing dialogue with them, and is the relationship effectively managed?

Legitimacy grants the organization the right to operate or to continue operating; in such a way that when stakeholders perceive that organizations are not acting in good faith, or their practices are unethical or questionable, they may find themselves at the center of discussions about their permanency in the market. Conversely, when stakeholders consider that the organization is operating in alignment with their moral compass, as well as with the enterprise's statements, stakeholders support the organization rather than create barriers or obstacles to operate. Since organizations cannot operate without the participation of their stakeholders, ensuring their positive impact and influence is essential to goal achievement. Thus, ignoring what stakeholders have to say, whether a one-on-one suggestion or public statement (in person or online), would be unproductive, as the backlash of ignoring them may have worse consequences than their original concerns.

Considering that creating value entails perceived benefit for the associated cost, price, investment, or stake, added value suggests surpassing their expectations of the perceived benefits for the same associated outlay, interest, or stake. Of course, it is important to create value for stakeholders for the survival of any organization, however, the key to effective stakeholder management is to strive for the co-creation of added value. Meaning that it requires the active and proactive participation of the enterprise as well as other internal and external stakeholders.

Stakeholders' Actions Toward Social Development

An unfortunate misconception is that social problems only affect a particular number of people globally or certain segments of populations; it is a false impression, which further exacerbates the problems at hand as social issues, in fact, affect everyone to some degree or another. Therefore, the first step when taking action is the acknowledgment that social issues are all of our issues, and just because the effects are indirect does not exempt us from proactive action to achieve social justice and sustainable development. Social problems are complex and interconnected, with multiple contributing factors. For such matter, their resolution requires collective acknowledgment and action. In order to positively impact social development, it is imperative to address the social issues that continue to pervade society, locally, nationally, and globally, with critical objectives and a strategic plan to eradicate them.

It is quite likely that everyone knows at least one person from different generations that believes that theirs was the social justice generation. This is understandable as, for one, history is plagued with injustice and inequality, meaning that there has not been a generation that has been free, safe, healthy, or enjoyed a high quality of life in its entirety. Further, there have been leaders in each generation that have spearheaded important movements, propelled by determined and energetic followers, that have resulted in significant change which has transcended and informed the beliefs and behavior of the following generations. While each generational cohort has faced particular challenges, the ails that permeate society, unfortunately, prevail from one generation to another. It seems that every year we hear statements such as *things are getting worse*, *this year is worse than last year*, or *we were better off in my day*, in relation to safety, health, the environment, poverty, housing, and the economy, amongst other aspects.

From the social enterprise's standpoint, addressing social problems requires a comprehensive and multifaceted approach that involves all stakeholders taking action to raise awareness, influence public policy, mobilize community initiatives and, of course, impact business policies and standards. Social enterprises can advocate for change through their industrial relations, more specifically, by associating with other organizations that take a strong stance on and similar approach to social development. By doing so, they are able to create a sustainable and socially responsible supply chain which can, in turn, positively impact social change and enhance global social development.

There are four categories of actions that social enterprise stakeholders (i.e., the third group of people in action) take or can take in relation to social development, these being: stagnant, shuffling, stimulating, and shifting. Figure 3.1 includes a matrix of the 4Ss of stakeholder action for social development. The matrix includes four quadrants showing four degrees of stakeholder action related to the intensity of their voice (i.e., in terms of force and volume) and action, from low to high.

The lower left quadrant—stagnating—refers to those exhibiting low or no voice, and low or no action. Stakeholders that take a stagnant position depict lack of movement and, therefore, also lack of voice and action.

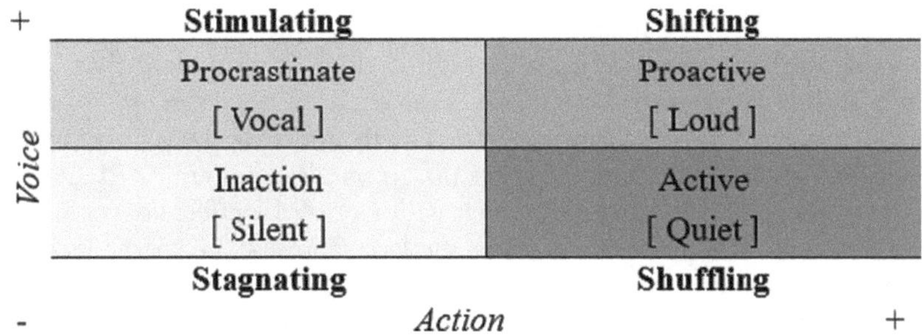

Fig. 3.1 4S matrix: stakeholder action for sustainable development

Their inactivity to foster growth or progress means that they do nothing to deter the negative effects on sustainable development. This does not mean that they are not aware of the social issues; moreover, their silence indicates that they do not object to the *status quo* or choose to ignore it as they extract benefits or obtain advantages from it, regardless of whether the gains are direct or indirect. Common examples include those who make statements such as *that's just the way things are/ the way things work*, *there is nothing I can do about it*, *it is not my responsibility*, etc. Therefore, stakeholders here choose to remain inactive and silent with respect to social and/or environmental issues.

The top left quadrant—stimulating—includes those individuals and/or organizations that display a high use of their voice, and low action. Stakeholders who adopt a stimulating position use their voice to encourage, incentivize, and/or promote growth and progress. That being said, it is much ado about nothing. Many mistakenly misinterpret the intensity of their voice, their loudness, or purposeful deliveries of their rhetoric about social change and sustainable development for actual action. Therefore, while their voices may be more consistent and louder than those stagnating, leading to their participation in raising awareness, they do not carry out positive change. Common examples include those that are certainly vocal, and take a strong public, frequently virtual, stance on a social issue; they indicate their indignation, however, they procrastinate when it is time to follow through. This posture, then, epitomizes individuals' cognitive dissonance, as well as organizations' corporate hypocrisy (Wagner et al., 2009). As such, their actions, or lack thereof, are well associated with practices such as greenwashing and social washing, amongst others.

The bottom right quadrant—shuffling—describes those stakeholders who show low use of voice and high action. Stakeholders that take on a shuffling position are typically associated with smaller or disorganized movements or actions toward growth and progress. Their voice regarding social issues is quiet as results are rarely communicated and, if known, they are often random. Their actions may be effective, yet there is a decrease in awareness regarding the latter's results given the lack of transparent communication. It is understandable that some may wish to remain anonymous in their actions, and avoiding self-praise is admirable, however, remaining quiet decreases awareness, accountability, as well as potential inspiration for other stakeholders to take action. Therefore, it is more difficult to build on their progress.

Finally, the top right quadrant—shifting—depicts the stakeholders that exhibit high use of their voice as well as high levels of action regarding social issues. The stakeholders that adopt a shifting position alter their mindset and standards of behavior to enable proactive participation in growth and progress. They voice their opinions and stance on social issues loudly and enthusiastically face-to-face as well as online, and proactively implement strategies and innovations to stimulate growth, as well as positive social change. Their intentions and results are transparently communicated, commonly boasted online, often positively impacting their image as ethical and socially responsible contributors to human and sustainable development.

Social enterprises' stakeholders, more likely than not, take on a shuffling or shifting position. Given the organization's social mission and profit-with-purpose approach to business, they are active or proactive in driving social change by tackling social and/or environmental issues having a negative impact on sustainable development. This makes sense since stakeholders have gradually demonstrated a preference to associate with organizations that exhibit involvement with the community (Amato and Amato, 2007), as well as environmental concerns (Bird et al., 2007). However, in terms of voicing their stance on social issues, they are in all probability displaying a shifting posture. Moreover, stakeholders in a shuffling or shifting position are also more likely to do so cooperatively.

Collective Behavior and Crowd Behavior

The third group of people in action in social enterprises often demonstrate their action collectively. In order to understand the implications of social movements, it is necessary to first understand the intricacies of collective behavior and crowd behavior. Collective behavior is descriptive as that of a large group of people that, while somewhat organized, is less organized, at least initially, than people's standard or typical behavior; furthermore, although prompted, collective behavior is frequently unplanned. There are many types of collective behavior, including but not limited to: crowds, mobs, mass hysteria, riots, and social movements, amongst others.

Crowd behavior, also known as mass behavior, by definition differs from individual behavior and is more often than not prompted by a social issue or event (Brindal et al., 2022). A crowd is a group of people that gathers at a certain physical location given a shared interest to achieve a particular objective. According to Al-Gadhi (1996), crowd behavior has certain characteristics, such as demographics, quorum, mood, and degrees of aggregation. Crowd behavior is typically associated with irrational behavior and/or violence; however, understanding collective behavior will depend on the theory used for its analysis.

There are many theories that scholars and researchers have developed over the years to explain collective behavior or crowd behavior. For instance, contagion theory, developed in 1895, suggests that when individuals are grouped as a crowd, they are prone to irrational behavior (Le Bon, 2006); this is commonly known as mob mentality. Convergence theory posits that crowds are not inherently violent; people converge with others who share the same ideas and objectives before engaging in collective behavior (Goode, 1992); in such a way that collective behavior only accentuates the individual's own beliefs and behavior, rather than being influenced by the crowd itself. According to Smelser (1962), value-added theory, also known as structural-strain theory, suggests that collective behavior such *as social movements* require some structural strain (i.e., certain factors that can lead to a specific type of collective event). In other words, there has to be a particular event or incident related to a social issue that, at the very least, frustrates a group of people based on the belief that the situation requires improving, preventing, or obstructing, and that the participants do not have an expectation of being penalized for their involvement.

Collective behavior, such as crowds, may originate with one person or a small group of people calling others to action. Therefore, it is common for collective behavior to begin in an unassuming manner, perhaps even underground, and grow gradually until a crowd is formed. For decades, crowds notoriously took to the streets to voice their outrage and demonstrate their discontent with a particular issue. However, although many groups proceed with the aforementioned approach, the Internet of Things (IoT), social media, and social networking sites have significantly changed the game, as these are now also used to foster collective behavior by calling to action, and creating crowds gathering virtually, that is, on online platforms; these crowds may remain online or, once organized, may also take to the streets to express their objectives and interests.

Stakeholders and Social Movements

Social movements are, then, a type of collective action of crowd behavior. Social movements are collective, organized efforts, planned and executed by groups of people who share an objective to generate change, which can be political, cultural (Staggenborg, 2016), economic, social, environmental, or political change. To be clear, social movements can either seek to bring about change or impede it as some are adamant about changing the existing state of affairs. They can have different forms including, but not limited to grassroots community efforts, large-scale mobilizations, organized campaigns, e-movements, and global movements, amongst others, which can have a local, national, and/or global reach. These movements are particularly important because they typically emerge in response to perceived injustices, inequalities, or grievances that systematically impede growth and development. Therefore, in such cases, they seek to challenge the *status quo* as well as transform existing power structures and societal norms.

Social movements may have various objectives such as social justice which targets issues such as discrimination, inequality, inequity, human rights violations, etc., policy change which seeks to influence regulatory authorities' policies, laws, and regulations, as well as lobbying efforts, and cultural shifts which intend to challenge current attitudes, beliefs, and behaviors. Therefore, social movements can focus on civil rights, the environment, labor, politics, and peace, amongst many other aspects. The inspiration for social movements is clear and they can form rather quickly, however, their success is far more complex. That is because a series of factors are required for their success, including strategic management (i.e., strategic planning, organizing, leading, as well as control mechanisms), infrastructure, resources, effective followership, and, importantly, stakeholders' support, participation, and activism.

The results of a social movement, when positive, bring about important social change; that being said, the longevity of the positive outcomes is often uncertain. It would seem that once an individual or group of people have been educated on a topic, that there is no way to uneducated them; this notion has contrasting implications. On the one hand, if true to form, once people have been educated on social and environmental issues, their behavior and attitudes would, theoretically, be adjusted accordingly and would remain as such throughout time. If this were straightforward, social movements would not require repetition. On the other hand, this would also mean that people are not capable of change and transformation, which is the main requirement for the success of a social movement, as well as growth and development.

Unfortunately, there are recent examples that demonstrate that important social change can be reversed when least expected. Multiple notable advances had been made previous to 2019, however, the effects of the COVID-19 pandemic have caused a series of social and environmental setbacks, particularly in developing countries such as those in Latin America and the Caribbean, such as increased poverty, extreme poverty, and hunger, climate change, war, and human rights violations, amongst others. Furthermore, political shifts have also proven to obstruct progress as well as growth and development, with the U.S. Supreme Court overturning Roe v Wade being case in point. In Latin America this has been witnessed with the privatization of natural resources, systematic reduction of investment in research and development, as well as censorship, forced disappearance, vote buying, and political trials, amongst many others; the likelihood of these actions is all the more probable given the region's historic background as discussed in Chapter 1.

Social movements in Latin America and the Caribbean have played a significant role in shaping the political, economic, social, and cultural landscape of the region. Just like in every other region, these movements have emerged in response to various social issues, including inequality, inequity, human rights violations, environmental problems, and political repression and oppression, amongst others. Throughout history, there have been multiple social movements in the region, such as farmers' movements, labor movements, and student movements (Bruckmann &

Dos Santos, 2006); some historic examples include the 1937 Labor Riots of the Trade Union Movement in Trinidad and Tobago (National Archives of Trinidad & Tobago, 2020), the Landless Workers' Movement (MST) in Brazil in 1984 (Carter, 2010), the Mexican student movement in 1968 (López, 2016), the Zapatista Movement in 1994 (Lomelí, 2023), the Mothers of the Plaza de Mayo in 1977 in Argentina (Femenía & Gil, 1987), the Chilean student movement in 2011 (Larrabure & Torchia, 2015), as well as various women's, environmental, and anticorruption movements, amongst many others.

However groundbreaking, some of the movements in Latin America and the Caribbean have reappeared over time; meaning that they have shown longevity and often require repetition within and across generations due to inadequate follow-through by decisionmakers and policymakers. One example is the environmental movement which addresses issues like climate change, pollution, global warming, and conservation. Despite significant awareness and advocacy, many policies aimed at protecting the environment often lack enforcement or commitment, necessitating ongoing activism and re-engagement from society, organizations, and stakeholders. Other examples include the civil rights movement, which continues to evolve and address ongoing disparities and injustices, and women's social movements in the region are also long-lasting and have evolved over the decades, addressing issues such as gender-based violence, femicide, reproductive rights, political representation, and economic inequality.

Activism includes the efforts and actions taken by individuals or groups of people to bring about change. Activists work toward promoting, impeding, directing, or intervening in social, political, economic, and/or environmental reform with the desire to make improvements in society; they are, therefore, essential stakeholders for social movements as well as for social enterprise's operations and performance. As such, activism requires being determined, poignant, persuasive, and steadfast in order to achieve individual and group objectives. It tends to be associated with extremists; however, this is a misconception typically confused with extremism. That is, activism entails action that is both legal and nonviolent (Leuprecht et al., 2020) while extremists more often than not violate others' rights as well as negatively affect their welfare (Kim, 2021). In fact, activists pursue their objectives by voicing their opinions and taking a stance and action against a particular local, national, or international issue that needs attention and significant reconsideration (Skaidrė,

2019) to improve well-being, deter the violation of human rights, stop environmental destruction, etc. The associated stakeholders would, then, be shifting in the social movement (see Fig. 3.1). As such, activists are both important and necessary for the effectiveness of the movement. Activists may employ different strategies to achieve their goals, such as advocacy, protests (both in person and online), civil disobedience (form of resistance; can be active, passive, direct, or indirect (Chong, 2001)), lobbying, community organizing, educational campaigns, and business campaigns, amongst others.

Women's movements, which are collective actions organized by and consisting of women to prompt social change (Ferree & Mueller, 2004), have been major disruptors in different points in history around the world. The Latin American political, social, cultural, and economic backgrounds have served as inspiration, resilience, as well as decisiveness to fight for what is right, at the very least fair. Women's movements in Latin America, like in other regions, have been particularly relevant to the associated countries' democratization, such as between the decade of the 1980s–1990s (Anderson, 2020), as well as the pursuit of others' rights. According to Safa (1990), women's movements in Latin America have largely centered on fighting repression and survival; however, just like around the world, they are also focused on achieving "justice, development and equality" (Bahous, 2022). It is quite remarkable how the majority of the world's population maintains a vulnerable status; women live in a constant state of oppression, insecurity, fear, inequality, inequity, and violence, regardless of their location around the world.

According to Anderson (2020), women's movements in Latin America and the Caribbean began in the late nineteenth century, with a particular focus on their civil status, labor rights, access to education, as well as the right to vote. Well into the third decade of the twenty-first century, women are mobilizing to ensure that they are safe, that their human rights are not violated, fair wages, and social justice, and equity in general. While collective action has reminded women that they have a voice worth listening to, it is also true that progress has been far too slow. Women continue to fight for the right to freedom, yes, even in declared democratic countries, women are still striving for their freedom to live without fear, to exist.

One of the most recent women's movements, which seeks to eradicate gender-based violence and femicide, has taken to social media and social networking sites; Rovira-Sancho and Morales-i-Gras (2022) found that three important hashtags were heavily used between 2015 and 2020 in Argentina, Mexico, and Spain, these being #NiUnaMenos (not one less woman), #Cuéntalo (tell it), and #NiUnaMas (not one more woman), respectively. They were used not only to mobilize groups of women, but also served as means to unite women internationally; in such a way that women activism in Latin America has expanded and now has an important online presence. It is noteworthy that women's movements can have consequences that overflow to other important social issues; for instance, they impact education, political and legal rights, and cultural norms; a positive impact on these can, in turn, positively impact issues related to poverty, social health, and housing, amongst others.

All social movements are possible due to stakeholder participation and activism. Despite the fact that there is an extensive history of activism and social movements in Latin America and the Caribbean, many have stayed away from actively participating in social movements, at least in person. One of the main reasons why some individuals are reluctant to participate is fear of repercussion either from government authorities or organizational leaders (i.e., being fired from their current jobs or not being hired), mainly due to a demonstration of opposition as well as the fact that activists, such as protestors, may be mistakenly viewed as irrational participants or instigators (another protected effect of the region's historical background). This is also associated with the level of credibility ascribed to those in authoritative positions who make assertions about the reality of social growth and development as well as social movement participants.

When crowd behavior, such as social movements, is associated merely with irrational behavior, social inequity is exacerbated. Near the end of the 1960s, Howard Becker coined the concept of hierarchy of credibility (Becker, 1967) which conveys the effects of social inequalities. It describes a phenomenon that occurs within a hierarchical system or organization where higher-ranking members or those with greater authority are deemed credible without significant delay given their position. There is an assumption that those at the top have clarity of information, access to accurate data, and overall greater knowledge than lower-ranking members; in such a way that those at the top are considered to be deserving of being heard and their assertions can be trusted, and vice versa for those lower-ranking members.

So, when individuals with power and authority relay information regarding, for instance, social development as well as social movements, others tend to believe it. This, again, goes back to colonialism and dictatorships in Latin America and the Caribbean, where a state and system of hierarchization was instilled which has never been eradicated, bringing about a persistent hierarchy of credibility. In any case, stakeholders' resistance to participate in social movements in person does not necessarily reflect their lack of interest but can be an effect of the perception of hierarchy of credibility. In consideration of these and other potential restrictions, social enterprises may serve as a conduit to bridge discontent with the current state of affairs and collaborative change.

Collaborative Change and Social Enterprises

Organizations have gradually increased their participation in activism by stating support for movements such as gun control and laws, Black Lives Matter (BLM), LGBTQ + , Cancer awareness, Urban waters movement, and health policies, amongst others. While they take a public stance on the matters (Fan, 2019), in many instances it is unclear if they do so because of an innate need to influence social change or if they merely do so to decrease the possibility of stakeholder backlash for remaining stagnant or taking a stimulating posture (see Fig. 3.1). Further, the lack of action and/or substance of action is, then, deemed as social washing (Rizzi et al., 2020), greenwashing (Yu et al., 2020), rainbow washing (Carbonell, 2021), pinkwashing (Lubitow & Davis, 2011), as well as CSR washing (Koleva & Meadows, 2021), etc., as a depiction of their cognitive dissonance. Therefore, organizations must not only be genuine in their dynamics related to social change but should also be able to successfully convey their efforts authentically to their current and potential stakeholders.

When social enterprises align with stakeholder theory, their stakeholders' interests, they are ultimately stating that their decision-making takes into consideration a series of variables that go beyond their bottom line. With stakeholder theory, developing strategies that make *good business sense* means driving business growth and development without sacrificing the needs, wants, and prosperity of the other interested parties. Doing so requires awareness of the social movements occurring in their community, at least the community surrounding their operations. It may be that they take on the social issue as part of the core business and social mission, or that they acknowledge their efforts and support them; either way, social entrepreneurs take a particular interest in social movements.

The vast social needs in Latin America and the Caribbean not only increase the existence and persistence of social movements, but also of social enterprises. The latter, along with stakeholders' growing concern for the issues that permeate societies, are a clear indication of the vast needs that the region continues to have to ensure sustainable development. Social enterprises, therefore, should (*i*) take inspiration from social movements and activists, and (*ii*) take a proactive stance on social movements by expanding on their advocacy and leaning into activism, that is, a shifting position. In other words, they go beyond merely stating that their actions are in support of or promoting a cause or social change. They not only understand the intricacies of the social issue in question, but also take proactive action to work toward social change by engaging with the enterprise's stakeholders who are at least voicing their intentions, if not equally interested in bringing about significant change. Thus, collaborative change may be effectively prompted by the cooperation and collaboration of social enterprises and their current and potential stakeholders. Moreover, the co-creation of value, which is discussed in the next chapter, is possible because of the third group of people in action in social enterprises.

References

Al-Gadhi, A. A. H. (1996). A review study of crowd behavior and movement. *Journal of King Saud University - Engineering Sciences, 8*(1), 77–107. https://doi.org/10.1016/S1018-3639(18)30641-X

Amato, L. H., & Amato, C. H. (2007). The effects of firm size and industry on corporate giving. *Journal of Business Ethics, 72*(3), 229–241. https://doi.org/10.1007/s10551-006-9167-5

Anderson, C. F. (2020). Latin American women's movements: A historical overview. In X. Xóchitl Bada, & L. Rivera-Sánchez, (Eds). *The Oxford Handbook of the Sociology of Latin America* (pp. 339–356). https://doi.org/10.1093/oxfordhb/9780190926557.013.22

Bahous, S. (2022). *Moving forward*. UN Women. Retrieved November 29th, 2023, from: https://www.unwomen.org/en/annual-report/2022

Becker, H. S. (1967). Whose side are we on? *Social Problems, 14*(3), 239–247. https://doi.org/10.2307/799147

Bird, R., Hall, A. D., Momentè, F., & Reggiani, F. (2007). What corporate social responsibility activities are valued by the market? *Journal of Business Ethics, 76*(2), 189–206. https://doi.org/10.1007/s10551-006-9268-1

Brindal, E., Kakoschke, N., Reeson, A., & Evans, D. (2022). Madness of the crowd: Understanding mass behaviors through a multidisciplinary lens. *Frontiers in Psychology, 13*, 4. https://doi.org/10.3389/fpsyg.2022.924511

Bruckmann, M., & Dos Santos, T. (2006). *Los movimientos sociales en América Latina: Un balance histórico.* CETRI. Retrieved October 22nd, 2023, from: https://www.cetri.be/Los-movimientos-sociales-en?multi=multi&lang=fr

Buchholz, H., Eberle, T., Klevesath, M., Jürgens, A., Beal, D., Baic, A., & Radeke, J. (2020). Forward thinking for sustainable business value: A new method for impact valuation. *Sustainability, 12*(20), 8420. https://doi.org/10.3390/su12208420

Carbonell, N. (2021). *What is rainbow washing? (and how to avoid it in your company).* Business. Retrieved August 5th, 2023, from: https://www.sfgate.com/business/article/What-is-rainbow-washing-and-how-to-avoid-it-in-16349603.php

Carroll, A. B. (2004). Managing ethically with global stakeholders: A present and future challenge. *Academy of Management Perspectives, 18*(2), 114–120. https://doi.org/10.5465/ame.2004.13836269

Carter, M. (2010). The landless rural workers movement and democracy in Brazil. *Latin American Research Review, 45*, 186–217. https://doi.org/10.1353/lar.2010.0032

Chithambo, L., Tauringana, V., Tingbani, I., & Achiro, L. (2022). Stakeholder pressure and greenhouses gas voluntary disclosures. *Business Strategy and the Environment, 31*(1), 159–172. https://doi.org/10.1002/bse.2880

Chong, D. (2001). Political protest and civil disobedience. In N. J. Smelser, P. B. Baltes, & P.B. (Eds.), *International encyclopedia of the social & behavioral sciences* (pp. 11693–11696). Elsevier Ltd.

Donaldson, T., & Preston, L. E. (1995). The stakeholder theory of the corporation: Concepts, evidence, and implications. *The Academy of Management Review, 20*(1), 65–91. https://doi.org/10.2307/258887

Eesley, C., & Lenox, M. J. (2006). Firm responses to secondary stakeholder action. *Strategic Management Journal, 27*(8), 765–781. https://doi.org/10.1002/smj.536

Fan, J. S. (2019). Woke Capital: The role of corporations in social movements. *Harvard Business Law Review, 9*, 441–494. https://digitalcommons.law.uw.edu/faculty-articles/586

Femenía, N. A., & Gil, C. A. (1987). Argentina's mothers of Plaza de Mayo: The mourning process from junta to democracy. *Feminist Studies, 3*(1), 9–18. https://doi.org/10.2307/3177832

Fernández, A. M. L., & Rajagopal, N. A. (2014). Convergence of corporate social responsibility and business growth: An analytical framework. *International Journal of Business Excellence, 7*(6), 791–806. https://doi.org/10.1504/IJBEX.2014.065508

Ferree, M. M., & Mueller, C. M. (2004). Feminism and the women's movement: A global perspective. In D. A. Snow, S. A. Soule, & H. Kriesi (Eds.), *The Blackwell companion to social movements* (pp. 576–607). Blackwell Publishing.

Freeman, R. E. (1984). *Strategic management: A stakeholder approach*. Pitman.

Freeman, R. E., Harrison, J. S., Wicks, A. C., Parmar, B. L., & de Colle, S. (2010). *Stakeholder theory: The state of the art*. Cambridge University Press.

Freeman, R. E., & Reed, D. L. (1983). Stakeholder and stockholder: A new perspective on corporate governance. *California Management Review, 25*(3), 88–106. https://doi.org/10.2307/41165018

Friedman, M. (1962). *Capitalism and freedom*. Chicago: University of Chicago. Press and Pheonix Books.

Friedman, M. (2007). The social responsibility of business is to increase its profits. In W. C. Zimmerli, M. Holzinger, & K. Richter (Eds.), *Corporate ethics and corporate governance*. Springer.

Goode, E. (1992). *Collective behavior*. Harcourt Brace Jovanovich.

Greenley, G. E., & Foxall, G. R. (1996). Consumer and nonconsumer stakeholder orientation in U.K. companies. *Journal of Business Research, 35*(2), 105–116. https://doi.org/10.1016/0148-2963(95)00052-6

Gaur, V. (2013). Understand your stakeholders. *International Journal of Advancements in Research & Technology, 2*(1), 1–8.

Hill, C. W. L., & Jones, T. M. (1992). Stakeholder-agency theory. *Journal of Management Studies, 29*(2), 131–154. https://doi.org/10.1111/j.1467-6486.1992.tb00657.x

Kim, S. C. (2021). *Extremist mindsets and strategies*. McFarland & Company, Inc., Publishers.

Koleva, P., & Meadows, M. (2021). Inherited scepticism and neo-communist CSR-washing: Evidence from a post-communist society. *Journal of Business Ethics, 174*, 783–804. https://doi.org/10.1007/s10551-021-04929-7

Langtry, B. (1994). Stakeholders and the moral responsibilities of business. *Business Ethics Quarterly, 4*(4), 431–443. https://doi.org/10.2307/3857342

Larrabure, M., & Torchia, C. (2015). The 2011 Chilean student movement and the struggle for a new left. *Latin American Perspectives, 42*(5), 248–268. https://doi.org/10.1177/0094582X14547506

Le Bon, G. (2006). *The crowd: A study of the popular mind*. Cosimo Inc.

Leuprecht, C., Skillicorn, D. B., & McCauley, C. (2020). Terrorists, radicals, and activists: Distinguishing between countering violent extremism and preventing extremist violence, and why it matters. In S. von Hlatky (Ed.), *Countering violent extremism and terrorism: Assessing domestic and international strategies* (pp. 18–46). McGill-Queens University Press.

Light, P. C. (2009). Social entrepreneurship revisited. *Stanford Social Innovation Review, 7*(3), 21–22. https://doi.org/10.48558/Z8K2-W870

Lomelí, C. B. Z. (2023). El movimiento zapatista y la transición democrática en México: Oportunidades para la movilización, el éxito y la supervivencia. *Estudios Sociológicos de El Colegio de México, 41*(121), 275.

López, A. C. (2016). Movimiento del 68: el origen de la dualidad política en México. *Tla-melaua. Revista de las Ciencias*. 10(40), 197–206. Retrieved August 2nd, 2023 from: https://www.scielo.org.mx/pdf/tla/v10n40/1870-6916-tla-10-40-00196.pdf

Lubitow, A., & Davis, M. (2011). Pastel Injustice: The corporate use of pinkwashing for profit. *Environmental Justice, 2*(2), 139–144. https://doi.org/10.1089/env.2010.0026

Nash, R. F. (1990). *The rights of nature. A history of environmental ethics*. Primavera Press.

National Archives of Trinidad and Tobago. (2020). *Tubal Uriah "Buzz" Butler. The man and his times*. Office of the Prime Minister - Communications. Retrieved November 2nd, 2023, from: https://www.natt.gov.tt/sites/default/files/pdfs/ButlerRevisedBoards11June.pdf

Orts, E. W., & Strudler, A. (2002). The ethical and environmental limits of stakeholder theory. *Business Ethics Quarterly, 12*(2), 215–233. https://doi.org/10.2307/3857811

Phillips, R. A., & Reichart, J. (2000). The environment as a stakeholder? A fairness-based approach. *Journal of Business Ethics, 23*(2), 185–197. https://doi.org/10.1023/A:1006041929249

Phillips, R., Freeman, R. E., & Wicks, A. C. (2003). What stakeholder theory is not. *Business Ethics Quarterly, 13*(4), 479–502. https://doi.org/10.5840/beq200313434

Ramus, T., & Vaccaro, A. (2017). Stakeholders matter: How Social enterprises address mission drift. *Journal of Business Ethics, 143*, 307–322. https://doi.org/10.1007/s10551-014-2353-y

Rizzi, F., Gusmerotti, N., & Frey, M. (2020). How to meet reuse and preparation for reuse targets? Shape advertising strategies but be aware of "social washing." *Waste Management, 101*, 291–300. https://doi.org/10.1016/j.wasman.2019.10.024

Rovira-Sancho, G., & Morales-i-Gras, J. (2022). *Femitags* for feminist connected crowds in Latin America and Spain. *Acta Psychologica 230*, 103756. https://doi.org/10.1016/j.actpsy.2022.103756

Safa, H. I. (1990). Women's social movements in Latin America. *Gender and Society. Special Issue: Women and Development in the Third World, 4*(3), 354–369. https://doi.org/10.1177/089124390004003006

Savage, G. T., Nix, T. W., Whitehead, C. J., & Blair, J. D. (1991). Strategies for assessing and managing organizational stakeholders. *Academy of Management Perspectives, 5*(2), 61–75. https://doi.org/10.5465/ame.1991.4274682

Sekliuckiene, J., & Kisielius, E. (2015). Development of social entrepreneurship initiatives: A theoretical framework. *Procedia - Social and Behavioral Sciences, 213*, 1015–1019. https://doi.org/10.1016/j.sbspro.2015.11.519

Skaidrė, Ž. (2019). Grassroots activism and sustainable development. In W. Leal Filho (Ed.), *Encyclopedia of sustainability in higher education*. Springer.

Smelser, N. J. (1962). *Theory of collective behavior*. Free Press.

Smith, L., & Woods, C. (2015). Stakeholder engagement in the social entrepreneurship process: Identity, governance and legitimacy. *Journal of Social Entrepreneurship, 6*(2), 186–217. https://doi.org/10.1080/19420676.2014.987802

Staggenborg, S. (2016). *Social movements*. Oxford University Press.

Starik, M. (1995). Should trees have managerial standing? Toward stakeholder status for non-human nature. *Journal of Business Ethics, 14*(3), 207–217. https://doi.org/10.1007/BF00881435

Thornock, B. O. S. (2016). A strategic stakeholder approach for addressing further analysis requests in whole genome sequencing research. *Life Sciences, Society and Policy, 12*(4), 1–7. https://doi.org/10.1186/s40504-016-0037-3

Wagner, T., Lutz, R. J., & Weitz, B. A. (2009). Corporate hypocrisy: Overcoming the threat of inconsistent corporate social responsibility perceptions. *Journal of Marketing, 73*(6), 77–91. https://doi.org/10.1509/jmkg.73.6.77

Weiss, J. W. (2014). *Business ethics: A managerial, stakeholder approach*. Berrett-Koehler Publishers Inc.

Yu, E.P.-Y., Van Luu, B., & Chen, C. H. (2020). Greenwashing in environmental, social and governance disclosures. *Research in International Business and Finance, 52*, 101192. https://doi.org/10.1016/j.ribaf.2020

CHAPTER 4

Co-Creating Value and Added Value Through Social Enterprises

Abstract Social enterprises are able to create and, importantly, co-create value for current and potential stakeholders, particularly the community they serve. The success of the enterprise's social mission significantly depends on the effectiveness of the shared responsibility of all stakeholders for the co-creation of added value. The latter may be achieved through an integral process including the evaluation of business models, environmental analysis, stakeholder management, social responsibility, and sustainable decision-making.

Keywords Value co-creation · Added value · Stakeholders · Business model · Social enterprise responsibility

Organizations, including social enterprises, are currently facing complexities both with historical parallels, as well as without precedent; in such a way that, within the third decade of the twenty-first century, the challenges management must tackle exceed the internal dynamics of business since these are informed by the environmental context that has more than proven to be turbulent, to say the least. The current reality demonstrates that societies' complexities are increasingly alarming, with implications in just about every sector, industry, and, of course, community. This is

A. M. López-Fernández, *Co-Creation in Social Enterprises*, Palgrave Studies of Entrepreneurship and Social Challenges in Developing Economies, https://doi.org/10.1007/978-3-031-83449-3_4

particularly true for emerging markets, and the reality of the challenges societies face in these markets is identified as a source of inspiration for social innovation. Social enterprises can create, more importantly, they can co-create value and added value for their stakeholders, particularly their beneficiaries, as well as deliver value in the form of growth and development. This chapter begins with a description of perceived and created value and added value and a discussion on the co-creation of value and added value by social enterprises and stakeholder participation. Then, a five-step process for co-creating added value through sustainable development is described, illustrating how groups two, three, and four of people in action in social enterprises interact and enrich desired results.

The fourth group of people in action is the social enterprise's beneficiaries, sometimes referred to as the community that benefits from the enterprise's operations and decisions which lead to the achievement of its dual mission. In order to achieve positive effects for the fourth group, the actions of groups two and three are also necessary. For instance, suppose that a social entrepreneur develops a dual mission that is associated with objectives for the reduction of poverty of a particular community, each of the organization's current stakeholders, which include the served community, are directly impacted by its business dynamics because they actively and proactively participate in the creation of the social enterprise's value and benefit from it. How well the mission is carried out will depend on the degree and effectiveness of the shared responsibility of all three groups of people in action in the social enterprise.

Shared Responsibility

Shared responsibility suggests that there are various parties participating in the achievement of a particular objective, completion of a project, development of working solutions for various social issues, amongst others. For instance, when facing a natural disaster, all members of society have certain responsibilities, and they should work together effectively toward decreasing the negative impact of the disaster (Lukasiewicz et al., 2017). It requires effective collaboration, meaning, the effective cooperation and coordination of the associated participants; the latter agree on the importance of their active participation and recognize that they are accountable to each other as well as other associated stakeholders. Further, those who take part will depend on the purpose of collaboration, and can be governments (leaders, organizations, institutions), private sector organizations, entrepreneurial organizations, non-governmental organizations (NGOs), as well as individuals. Shared responsibility has the power to prompt action and enhance positive results, as well as reduce costs and risks; therefore, there are significant benefits that can be particularly strategic for those involved.

There have been many leaders through the years all over the world that have made valiant efforts urging immediate action for substantial and transformational change, as easy as being kind to others, to eradicating systemic racisms, violence, inequality, hunger, and poverty, amongst others. Suffice it to say, these are not simple tasks, nor can they be resolved by a few willing to dedicate their lives' work to change. The challenges that societies in Latin America and the Caribbean face are multifaceted and, in order to positively impact social development, private and public organizations, in addition to individuals, need to share the responsibility of the region's growth and development. As has been discussed, social enterprises are particularly relevant when it comes to the proactive participation in societal prosperity.

There are many factors that impact the perpetuation of poverty, poor health, and inadequate housing. Historic factors, such as colonialism and dictatorships, mentioned in Chapter 1 have had a long-lasting effect on resource distribution, social hierarchies, and ownership, amongst others. Educational disparities and unequal access to opportunities limit the possibility of marginalized groups escaping poverty. Healthcare disparities are visible via the lack of access to healthcare, malnutrition, and higher mortality rates, amongst others, which largely impact vulnerable sections of the population. Economic instability including income and wealth inequality, unfair wages, unemployment, informal economy, commodity price fluctuations, and inflation, amongst others, significantly limit access to economic opportunities, and disproportionately affect the middle to bottom of the population's pyramid. Lack of access to infrastructure and basic services, job insecurity, crime, and violence also negatively impact poverty. And, even more troubling given the degree of embeddedness in governance, corruption, and impunity certainly impact the effectivity of public institutions and organizations that seek to reduce poverty and improve social well-being and development. Therefore, tackling the root causes and effects of poverty and extreme poverty, poor social health, and inadequate housing, requires addressing the structural inequalities from various avenues. It is not surprising that the various crises that societies have endured have led to entrepreneurship, particularly social entrepreneurship, being perceived as a solution, as these enterprises may help clearly identify social needs, as well as create significant social change (Solano et al., 2017).

Understandably, many have and will continue to argue that tending to society's development and welfare is a responsibility that falls under the purview of each country's government and associated regulatory authorities. And it makes sense to the extent that they are technically in charge of public policy, fiscal administration, infrastructure development, and administration of the public sector, amongst others, in order to drive economic growth and human development. According to the WHO (2023), governments are responsible for the health of their societies. According to International human rights law, governments must promote and protect human rights, as well as their fundamental freedoms (UN, 2020). However true, as unfortunate as it is, governments are unable to tend to their entire populations' needs effectively and optimally, particularly of those that have been historically overlooked, like in countries in Latin America and the Caribbean. The reality is that governments, especially those in emerging markets and developing countries, are rarely able to provide effective institutions, policy, and infrastructure to effectually serve entire populations; furthermore, political instability, economic uncertainty, insecurity, and, more recently, health issues such as the COVID-19 pandemic, naturally lead governments' agendas while other human development variables and indicators are pushed further down in their day-to-day agendas.

The historic foundation, current conditions, along with estimated projections, are a clear indication that there is a pressing need for the proactive participation of more than governments and international organizations. Meaning that, for there to be a significant impact on sustainable development in the present and future, the responsibility must be shared with all types of organizations, institutions, as well as individuals. This may be observed via the social accountability, or lack thereof, displayed by all organizations, that is, public, private, for-profit, not-for-profit, as well as conventional businesses, entrepreneurial organizations, and social enterprises. A clear indication of social accountability is the acknowledgment of their responsibility in social growth and development, as well as the transparent communication of their policies, actions, and results.

While governments may find it particularly difficult to bring about substantial solutions for social problems, it is also true that public organizations are able to assist social entrepreneurs in their endeavors; they can do so by raising awareness of issues impacting society and the environment, assisting the entrepreneurs with resource procurement and coordination with other key public organizations, as well as helping with the execution of programs (Korosec & Berman, 2006) that may lead to advancements toward the achievement of the enterprise's dual mission; in such a way that public organizations and social enterprises may prosper in sharing responsibility for growth and development. Moreover, according to Waddock and Post (1991), an important distinction of social enterprises lies in the fact that their actions can directly impact public policy. This means that the independent actions of social enterprises as well as sharing responsibility with public organizations have a bidirectional effect; meaning that their actions directly, indirectly, and positively impact each other.

The social component of development is associated with individuals' active participation in the improvement of their quality of life (Roca, 2005). This suggests that individuals ought to participate, share responsibility, in their well-being and development. As such, social enterprise stakeholders, including their beneficiaries or communities they serve, should actively and proactively participate in achieving the dual mission in the pursuit of business and social growth and development. Sharing responsibility is, then, a matter for all groups of people in action in social enterprises, and also necessary to create value.

Perceived and Created Value and Added Value

There are two main ways in which value is defined, measured, and generated, these being financial value and perceived value (Boyles, 2022), both of which add value to the business itself, that is, in terms of its growth and development. Financial value is conceptualized as monetary value, the financial performance of the organization. It may be assessed in terms of capital, profit, income, return on investment, market share, and business growth in general. The better the financial performance, the greater the value (Boyles, 2022) for the organization as well as for its stakeholders, regardless of their initial interests. The latter is particularly true for investors, shareholders, collaborators, suppliers, and regulatory authorities as the effect is more direct. Financial value may be generated as long as the organization continues to provide products and services that are well received in the market, clear a profit, and do so competitively. Of course, market reception is not only associated with the product and/or service provided because there are other factors that impact the level of acceptance such as brand and organizational performance.

Perceived value has been defined in many manners (Boksberger & Melsen, 2011) and approached from different points of view, however, it has been traditionally used as a marketing strategy. According to Tuncer et al., (2021), perceived value is a key element of brand equity; what and how consumers perceive value is, then, elemental to organizations' successful results. Perceived value has been discussed since the 1980s (see Zeithaml, 1988) and became of particular importance a decade later (Zauner et al., 2015). The concept has been defined as consumers' assessment of the worth of a product and/or service that an organization offers (Hellier et al., 2003); understanding what value is for consumers is relevant to their satisfaction as well as the organization's competitiveness (Lusch & Vargo, 2006). Competitiveness has been defined as an organization's capacity to offer better products than their competitors, both in terms of higher value and price, in order to achieve a financial performance that supersedes that of the competition (Louati, 2018), as well as stakeholders' expectations. Therefore, it is also organizations' ability to reach a desired level of profitability by means of increased productivity and market share (Filó, 2007).

All consumers, across supply chains (i.e., from the beginning, procurement, and up to end consumers), tend to expect certain benefits to be obtained by purchasing and/or consuming a product and/or service. Therefore, value can be described as a consumer's perception of met expectations of the benefits of purchasing and/or consuming the product and/or service in relation to the cost incurred. In other words, it may easily be assessed as a cost–benefit analysis. While providing and obtaining value is important to the interested parties, its determination is, more often than not, prone to subjectivity and, therefore, cannot be assumed that it will be accepted as such or replicated across the board. There are many reasons for this; for instance, it does not necessarily matter whether the consumer's expectation of value is higher or lower than that of other consumers; meaning that value can be, and mostly is, a subjective aspect of decision-making and their perception which can vary from one consumer to another. Consumers' previous experiences with the same or similar products and services can also influence their perceptions of value. Furthermore, the intrinsic and extrinsic properties of products and services, while important variables, are not weighed the same in terms of importance or determinants of consumers' decision-making process.

Added value may be observed when consumers, and all stakeholders in general, perceive that their expectations of the benefits of purchasing and/or consuming the products and/or services are exceeded in relation to the cost incurred. Perceived added value has a direct impact on the organization's competitive advantage (de Chematony et al., 2015), not only for the organization's marketing and management strategies, but also for their business models (Zauner et al., 2015). Therefore, designing and executing strategies that foster added value becomes highly relevant to the achievement of organizations' desired performance.

Price and quality used to be the greatest determinants in consumer satisfaction and, therefore, in the perceived purchase or consumption value. However, the increase in alternatives on the market, advances in technology, the environmental context, and the overall movement of consumers' moral compass, amongst other aspects, have increased the variety of elements currently considered by consumers in their purchase decision-making process. There are many aspects and attributes that drive purchase decision-making and, therefore, may influence the perception of value and added value, including but not limited to product quality (Yoo & Sarin, 2018), degree of sacrifice (Agarwal & Teas, 2001), price (Sinha & Batra, 1999), degree of convenience (Singh et al., 2021), service quality and consumer satisfaction (Tuncer et al., 2021), engagement in corporate social responsibility (Al-Haddad et al., 2022), as well as sustainability (Verbeke et al., 2007). Having said that, it would be inaccurate to suggest that these actions are the norm, when, in fact, these are attitudes and behaviors of privileged consumers and other stakeholders; in other words, it is imperative to keep in mind that there is a significant proportion of the population around the world that while they might prefer to purchase from a socially responsible and sustainable organization that offers ethically manufactured and distributed products and/or services, if they are living paycheck to paycheck or in even more dire conditions, then, of course price is and will remain the strongest determinant in product, service, and brand selection. This alone is an important financial argument for enterprises involvement in social growth and development, as well as shared responsibility.

The fact is that all stakeholders, not just consumers, are continuously displaying a greater tendency toward organizations that fulfill a collection of needs that go beyond an affordable price and financial performance. As described in Chapter 3, stakeholders' voice is relevant to organizational leaders' decision-making, whether it be in relation to business dynamics, the products, and services the firm may offer, or their views as activists and participants of social movements (i.e., collective behavior and crowd behavior). Moreover, they are the third group in action in social enterprises and, for such matter, are essential to the co-creation of value as well as added value.

Co-Creating Value and Added Value

The co-creation of value is a business strategy that requires the active participation of all interested parties. It is a multidirectional process that requires synergy amongst the stakeholders who participate in the design, development, execution, and evaluation of value, as well as yields benefits for all parties involved. Also, co-creating value is plausible when synergy amongst the interested parties, stakeholders, is fostered and the enterprise's philosophy, culture, and governance, are aligned; in such a way that, by co-creating value, associated stakeholders receive what they want and need, and enterprises are able to meet their social objectives and, in turn, their dual mission. As such, instead of competing for a share of the value generated by an organization, stakeholders may actively contribute to the creation of the value as well as benefit from it. In other words, participate in the co-creation of value. When value is co-created, the recipients, beneficiaries, of social enterprise value are, then, those that participated in the process and the members of the served community. This means that co-creating value is fundamental to serving the fourth group of people in action in social enterprises, that is, the community that the enterprise is operating through and for; in a sense, those for whom the social mission was originally designed. For instance, engaging with communities is the manner by which social enterprise leaders, group two of people in action, are able to obtain key information and data regarding their needs and wants; in turn, they are able to forge and maintain relationships that will enable them to provide the necessary infrastructure as well as manage social development (Bice & Jones, 2022).

The synergetic process may be taken to the next level by being grounded in a strategic process for sustainable development based on future thinking and building, thereby working toward the co-creation of not just value but added value. Figure 4.1 illustrates the strategic process to co-create added value through sustainable development (CASD process). Future thinking and building entails steps whereby the enterprise designs, develops, and executes policies, objectives, and strategies

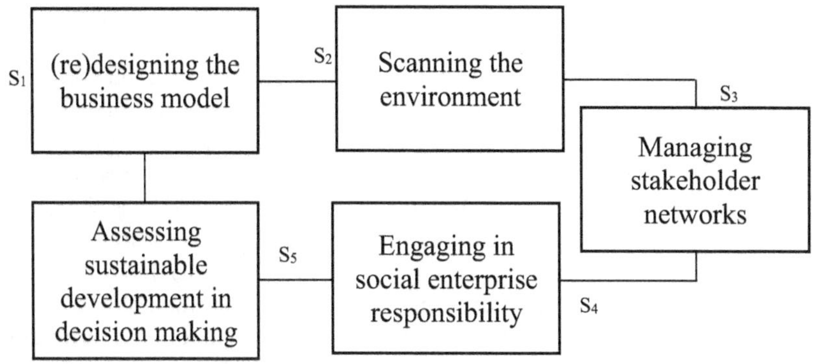

Fig. 4.1 Co-creating added value through sustainable development (CASD process)

that aim to address a community's current needs as well as those of people who may potentially find themselves with the same needs in the future, or, if at all possible, to eradicate the social issue they take on.

There are five steps that social enterprises may take in order to effectively co-create value and added value through sustainable development, including (S_1) (re)designing the business model, (S_2) scanning the environment, (S_3) managing stakeholder networks, (S_4) engaging in social enterprise responsibility, and (S_5) assessing sustainable development in the decision-making process. The CASD process is based on the premise that social enterprises use a profit-with-purpose approach that integrates sustainable development, as defined by the United Nations, into its business dynamics; therefore, there is a clear intent to provide for the current generation without compromising the prosperity of future generations. It is important to note that the steps are not necessarily carried out in the above-mentioned order, that is, the approach to the process will depend on the context and societal needs. For instance, in the beginning, it is likely that social entrepreneurs may decide to begin with step one, however, they will ideally eventually find themselves tackling all five steps simultaneously. The five steps are described in the following sections.

CASD Process: (Re)designing the Business Model

Innovation is necessary to ensure firms' survival (Dunne et al., 2016), therefore, developing an organizational climate and strategies fit for innovation are required in order to stimulate innovative attitude and behavior. Entrepreneurs are innovators; in fact, innovation is a distinctive entrepreneurship catalyst. According to Drucker (1985, p. 30), "It is the act that endows resources with a new capacity to create wealth". Furthermore, innovation is an important aspect to be considered in social enterprise success toward co-creating value through sustainable development. According to Boons et al., (2013, p. 1) "Sustainable development requires radical and systemic innovations". Doing so requires organizations to reengineer their processes and procedures and ensure that their commercial associates are aligned with their corporate philosophy, particularly their social mission; this means careful (re)consideration of their business model.

Social enterprises may produce substantial change regardless of their age as long as they are able to re-energize and revitalize the enterprise (Light, 2009), that is, their approach to business dynamics. Therefore, the first step in the co-creation of added value is designing or redesigning the social enterprise's business model. In order to ensure that the business model is aligned with the intention to co-create value, it should be inclusive; the objective is to create value for both the business and society while, for instance, including local communities in the business operations who would otherwise be overlooked, in order to incentivize economic growth by reducing poverty and enhancing overall social well-being. This can be done by designing a business model that is based on a circular economy.

A business model has the potential to positively influence an organization's generation of wealth (Zott & Amit, 2007). While business models are not in themselves strategies (Shafer et al., 2005), strategic thinking and action are required to design and execute them to achieve a strategic fit. Traditional business models use a linear type of system which begins with the exploitation of natural resources used for the production as well as distribution of products and ends with the end consumer who disposes of all or parts of the product purchased; as such, these models are clearly no longer sustainable.

Social enterprises' business models, as previously mentioned in Chapter 2, focus on staying in the market, being competitive, and covering their costs (Osorio-Novela et al., 2021). (Re)designing has the potential to transform this focus to a more strategic model that can better perform for all interested parties and toward the achievement of sustainable development. A business model based on circular economy, for instance, can recreate the market to serve social, environmental, and financial purposes. According to the European Parliament (2023), a circular economy uses business production and consumption models that entail extending the life cycle of products as well as materials; to do so, the model requires "sharing, leasing, reusing, repairing, refurbishing and recycling existing materials and products as long as possible"; in such a way that "all forms of waste are returned to the economy or used more efficiently" (UNCTAD, 2023). Social enterprises may benefit from a circular economy in many ways, for instance, it can help by increasing their levels of efficiency as their resources are sustainable and optimized, which also impacts the firm's cost reduction. These aspects certainly have a positive effect on the enterprise's business growth, which positively impacts its financial value. As processes are sustainable, there is a positive effect on social growth and development; moreover, achieving environmental development and sustainability will have a positive impact on society's health as well as quality of life (Bovarnick et al., 2010), therefore, well-being.

Another aspect that ought to be considered is focusing on social innovations which entails "the implementation of a new idea or initiative to change society in a fairer and more sustainable direction" (Gaiger et al., 2019, p. ii). Entrepreneurs are innovators (Drucker, 1985) and, according to Leadbeater (1997, p. 2), "social entrepreneurs will be one of the most important sources of innovation"; and, the latter is achieved by the intersection of public, private, and voluntary sector resources. Social enterprises are able to develop profit with purpose by creating products and services that, innovatively, tackle social issues that currently impede growth and development.

In Latin America and the Caribbean, the lack of innovation is a glaring deficiency in the entrepreneurial landscape (Lederman et al., 2014). Thus, (re)designing the business model requires social enterprise leaders to consider the manner in which it operates, the attributes of the products and/or services it offers, as well as the structure and efforts delegated toward innovation. Incidentally, a circular economy enables social enterprises to develop social innovations successfully.

CASD Process: Scanning the Environment

The second step in the process of co-creating value and added value through sustainable development is scanning the environment. This step requires social entrepreneurs to analyze the current social, political, and economic context of the country in question to be able to assess its level of sustainable development; therefore, this step requires both micro and macro analysis, that is, social enterprise leaders need to evaluate the social afflictions of the community they intend to serve as well as the associated variables in the country in order to understand the characteristics and implications, and the actions they need to take to tackle the issue. In the case of Latin America and the Caribbean, as mentioned in Chapter 1, social development is a particular concern; thus, considering the implications of poverty, health, and housing in the region is elemental to understanding the current state of the region.

As previously discussed, social entrepreneurs are concerned with generating social output, particularly in relation to society's welfare and health (Leadbeater, 1997). Therefore, social enterprises have the ability to impact communities' poverty, health, and housing directly and positively. As described in Chapter 1, all three aspects are significant areas of opportunity in Latin America and the Caribbean, and are interrelated; meaning that, a decrease/increase in one will positively/negatively impact the other two. For instance, health inequity exacerbates poverty and impedes access to housing or adequate housing, and the lack of promotion and assurance of housing is not only detrimental to individuals' welfare but is also a strong determinant of poverty and poor health.

In terms of poverty, according to Castelán et al., (2023), "a third of Latin American and Caribbean people are not poor, but they live one shock away from being brought back into poverty". This means that a slight or drastic shift in their current context, whether it be at a micro or macro level, could lead them into poverty. As we witnessed during the COVID-19 pandemic, this reality is all too familiar. How many people suddenly found themselves without income because they, unable to work due to illness or layoffs, lost their jobs? How many of them were unable to keep their homes, and access basic needs? And, how many found themselves living on or under the poverty or extreme poverty line? The fact is that any type of crisis or disaster has the potential to push people already in precarious conditions over the edge. As was discussed in Chapter 1, Latin America and the Caribbean region is a focal point for natural disasters, as well as social, political, environmental, and economic crises; in such a way that taking action to reduce and eradicate poverty must include those that are already living in dire conditions as well as creating a strategic plan that can mitigate the effects of such a shock, as well as prevent unnecessary adverse effects. To be clear, unnecessary effects are those that could be somewhat prevented or prepared for. While the COVID-19 pandemic might not have been explicitly preventable, the possibility of suddenly not being able to operate at capacity is a plan that all governments, organizations, and individuals (on the basis of their access to opportunities and basic needs), should have been able to design.

According to the Office of Disease Prevention and Health Promotion, there is a series of aspects that determine the health of individuals which, in turn, have a direct impact on their welfare and their quality of life, these being: "safe housing, transportation, and neighborhoods, racism, discrimination, and violence, education, job opportunities, and income, access to nutritious foods and physical activity opportunities, polluted air and water, and language and literacy skills" (OASH, 2023). In Latin America and the Caribbean, the fact that there is significant inequality in terms of access to health services is particularly discernable in the most vulnerable (WHO, 2023a), that is, those living in poverty or extreme poverty, and with limited or no access to basic services and the essentials to satisfy their basic needs. Further, over a decade ago, in 2012, Bouillon stated that the housing issue in Latin America and the Caribbean required a long-term sustainable solution; moreover, he ascertained that governments did not have the means or resources to do so effectively (BID, 2012). Therefore, additional assistance is required to generate such sustainable solutions in the region, which social enterprises may provide. Furthermore, clarity on the strategic plan to bring about change requires shared responsibility as well as a close relationship with all interested parties so as to be able to collect real-time data and information regarding the issue in question.

CASD Process: Managing Stakeholder Networks

The third step in the process of co-creating value and added value through sustainable development is managing stakeholder networks. All organizations, institutions, and companies are able to operate and fulfill their objectives because of the active participation of individuals and other organizations, stakeholders, with a specific, and perhaps varying, degree of interest in their results and impact on social growth and development. As mentioned in the previous chapter, stakeholder voice and action vary in relation to their stance on social development; in addition, achieving effective stakeholder management requires taking into consideration other key aspects as well.

Meeting stakeholders' interests and concerns, therefore, is key to value creation, and more importantly, for the co-creation of value. The latter being particularly relevant for the effective performance of social enterprises. In order to co-create value, a tightly webbed social network, a stakeholder network if you will, is required whereby all interested parties have a clear role in the achievement of organizational goals, which should be effectively aligned with their interests and concerns. The functionality of these networks depends on the social enterprise's policies, standards, and norms for stakeholder management. In other words, the enterprise's underlying guidelines that describe and dictate how the organization will operate internally and externally. Stakeholder management may be taken to the next level if organizational leaders take into consideration not only their current stakeholders, but also their potential stakeholders, as this would entail managing a future comprehensive view of the conceivable growth and development of the organization and, therefore, society.

An effective stakeholder network consists of the social enterprise's current and potential stakeholders, whose interests converge with the organization's corporate philosophy (i.e., mission, vision, core values, strategic objectives, strategies, and tactics) (López-Fernández, 2020). Said convergence is managed by means of four main practices: stakeholder empowerment, engagement, voice, and dialogue. Figure 4.2 depicts the management of a stakeholder network. It is organizations' responsibility to drive the process of stakeholder management, in that they should make the first move to establish a relationship with their potential interested parties; once they are on board, organizational leaders may begin to delegate efforts toward the main practices. The process of managing a stakeholder network is ongoing, meaning that there is no point at which these practices should be neglected.

Stakeholder empowerment entails working toward effective collaboration whereby participants believe they are sufficiently equipped and willing to take an active and proactive role in the enterprise's strategic objective attainment. An organization can foster this by increasing stakeholders' awareness of their operations and encouraging them to play a part in or invest in its outcomes; in other words, by engaging with them.

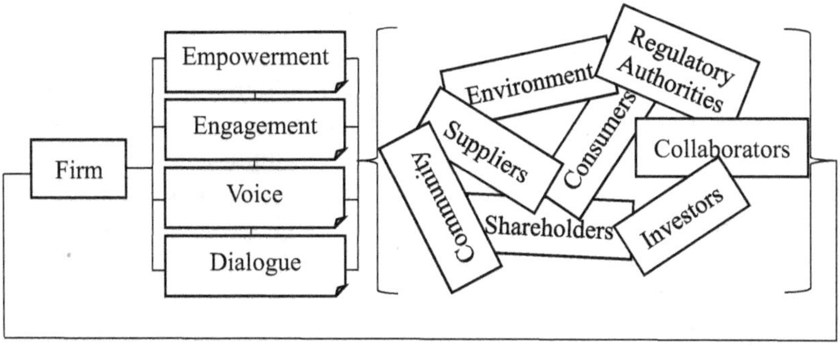

Fig. 4.2 Stakeholder network management

Stakeholder engagement in social enterprises is elemental to achieve successful outcomes; it has been defined as a process by which organizations involve stakeholders in the pursuit of their objectives and a manner of ensuring accountability (Leopizzi, 2020), in this case, social accountability which is derived from shared responsibility. It is achieved when interested parties are not only invested in the organization's results, but also cooperate and collaborate within their means and scope to influence and impact policies, strategies, operations, and, therefore, outcomes and performance. According to Ramus and Vaccaro (2017), internal and external stakeholder engagement is elemental to achieve optimal balance between the financial and social value; in other words, to attain desired social enterprise performance. Further, engagement is achieved by the effective management of stakeholder voice and dialogue (Leopizzi, 2020).

Stakeholder voice includes word-of-mouth (WOM) and, now with a greater probability, electronic word-of-mouth (eWOM). The Internet of Things (IOTs) (Sripriyanka & Mahendran, 2021) and, particularly, social media and social networking sites have increased the volume of stakeholder voice, both in terms of amount (i.e., quantity of accounts or users), and regarding resonance (i.e., quality or level of sound). It is important to note that social networking sites, such as Facebook, X (formerly Twitter), YouTube, TikTok, LinkedIn, etc., are boundless platforms with millions of active users, therefore, communication occurring on social media has a global reach; this means that organizational leaders need to be particularly vigilant of stakeholders' voice on said platforms. Moreover, stakeholder voice is also a clear indicator of their position and action for sustainable development (see Fig. 3.1), which is particularly relevant in the management of shared responsibility.

Stakeholder dialogue entails the organization's transparent disclosure and communication of its policies, actions, and results, actively listening to stakeholders' voice, and timely response to their input and contributions. More specifically, it means creating an environment where the organization's stakeholders feel heard, as opposed to merely recognizing what they have said, which only requires repeating their statements either back to them or publicly, in person or on a virtual platform. Social networking sites (SNSs) are ubiquitous and ideal platforms to engage in stakeholder dialogue; Latin America and the Caribbean has over five hundred million Internet users and is the fifth largest social media market (Bianchi, 2023), making these platforms a preferred source of communication, especially for younger generations.

Tending to all stakeholders at the same time and with the same degree of priority is not feasible. First, each decision will naturally require prioritizing some stakeholders over others; this arrangement is not done by ranking the importance of stakeholders, rather by ranking the relevance of the situation/decision at hand. And, doing so is not, or should not be, reflected in the overall work toward value co-creation; and second, attempting to tend to all stakeholders at the same time may be a cause for organizational inefficiency as well as conflicts (Banks, 2004) both internally and externally. Of course, efforts should be delegated to tending to any existing or potential conflict optimally, whether internal or external; however, integrating stakeholder interests and concerns into the organization's foundation, its corporate philosophy, also means that they are elemental to the organization's strategic management which will, in turn, determine the situations and manner in which each stakeholder will be prioritized.

The network may include local, national, as well as international stakeholders; therefore, the interested parties will depend on the organization's current scope of operation. The network's participants may also vary in terms of their intentions and delegated efforts toward: expansion (i.e., geographically; moving into additional locations (Barringer & Greening, 1998)), growth (i.e., in terms of profitability, competitiveness, market share, and volume of business (Fernández & Rajagopal, 2014), and scalability (i.e., the capability and capacity to grow and expand; and doing so by maintaining the same or greater level of efficiency (Jabłoński, 2016)). Since social enterprises vary in size, which is often influenced by their specific social mission, the social and/or environmental issue it aims to tackle, and the resources it has at its disposal, there is no particular starting point for expansion, growth, or scalability; that being said, the practices should remain the same.

When social enterprises effectively manage their stakeholder network, they are able to obtain critical information and data regarding their needs and wants, which means that the enterprise is better equipped to provide appropriate products and/or services. Using social networking sites not only allows firms to gather critical information and data directly from the source, but also enables gathering information and data in real-time, thus, enhancing the strategy as well as accuracy of their decisions. Enterprises are also able to understand stakeholders' views on and participation in social movements and activism, which can provide important insights into the social issues that need tending to (i.e., issue at hand as well as degree of urgency) and, in turn, inform their corporate philosophy. And they are able to create innovative solutions that drive social and environmental prosperity. As such, managing stakeholder networks is an important step in co-creating added value for the sustainable development of, at least, the community the enterprise is serving. The aforementioned effects are potentiated when social enterprises consider not just current stakeholders but also potential stakeholders, continuously.

CASD Process: Engaging in Social Enterprise Responsibility (SER)

The fourth step in the process of co-creating value and added value through sustainable development is engaging in social enterprise responsibility (SER), which derives from corporate social responsibility (CSR). In fact, social enterprise, sustainable development, and social responsibility attributes intersect; Fig. 4.2 depicts how all three converge. As discussed in Chapter 2, corporate social responsibility is an approach to business dynamics which entails achieving competitive advantage by converging business and social growth and development with the active and proactive participation of their stakeholders. Thus, social enterprises that approach business from a profit-with-purpose perspective are well on their way to engaging in social enterprise responsibility. The main reason being that they are operating based on the premise that their mission should have a positive impact on society and the environment, and CSR's primary pillars are social, environmental, and financial performance; also, CSR has a strategic fit with inclusive business models such as circular economy. Therefore, it is not a stretch for social enterprises to integrate social responsibility into their business dynamics, thereby engaging in SER.

When organizations effectively align their social responsibility policies and objectives to the seventeen sustainable development goals, they are able to create a positive effect at a micro and macro level; that is, they may be able to enhance the communities' sustainable development, as well as have a significant impact on the country's "sustainable development, innovation, competitiveness, impunity, and human development, and, in turn, impact global sustainable development" (López-Fernández et al., 2022, p. 261). Moreover, stakeholders have, or can have, a direct impact on organizational leaders' decisions (Hristov et al., 2022), related to their ethical and socially responsible behavior. Their growing interest and concern for the social and environmental issues that permeate society have a direct impact on their preference to associate with organizations that are ethical, sustainable, and socially responsible; it also impacts their willingness to pay or invest more in firms that are socially responsible, as well as their decision to switch brands when they become aware that organizations are operating in a less than ethical manner. Further, as stakeholders share their experiences and perceptions in the form of WOM and/or eWOM related to their expectations of enterprises' behavior, their preferences may influence enterprises' decisions in relation to their social responsibility engagement.

In the majority of cases, said influence would be tending toward a more ethical behavior, greater transparency of policies, actions, and results, and the maximization of positive effects on social, environmental, and financial performance. Since stakeholders are active and proactive participants in SER engagement, then, the latter is significantly important to social enterprises' co-creation of value and added value. In terms of specific action, social responsibility can reduce poverty; according to Boyle and Boguslaw (2007), organizations may generate profit by means of the same activities that are aimed at reducing poverty. Also, firms' social performance derived from their CSR engagement can have a positive impact on poverty, as well as health, hunger, and education, amongst others (López-Fernández, 2015), which directly impacts adequate housing. Therefore, social enterprise responsibility can further strengthen their social mission as well as sustainable development objectives and strategies. As shown in Fig. 4.3, as social enterprises effectively manage their stakeholder network, engage in SER and align with sustainable development, they are able

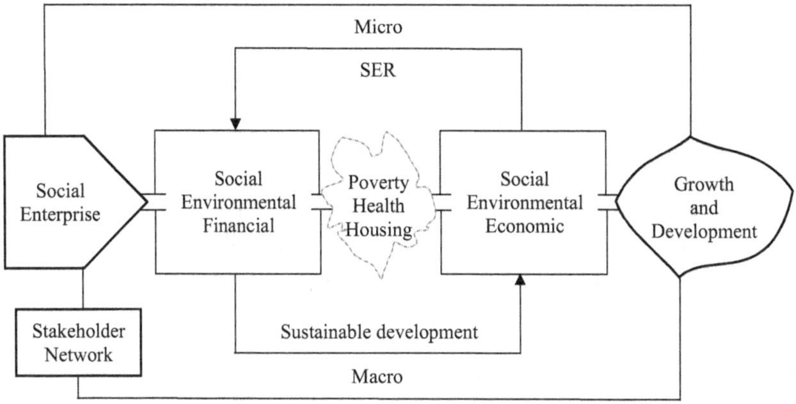

Fig. 4.3 Convergence of social enterprise, sustainable development, and SER

to impact poverty, health, and housing, amongst other aspects, and, in turn, impact the growth and development of the enterprise as well as that of their stakeholders. In other words, the figure describes the manner in which social enterprises' attributes serve as effective means to thrust social change toward social justice, for business and social growth and development. And value co-creation through social enterprises is not only able to drive successful outcomes by creating substantial value for their stakeholders in the form of social growth and development but can also promote the firm's financial performance and drive growth and scalability.

CASD Process: Assessing Sustainable Development in Decision-Making

The fifth step in the process of co-creating value and added value through sustainable development is assessing sustainable development in the enterprise's decision-making process. In addition to incorporating sustainable development in the enterprise's decision-making, this step also requires assessing how effective the impact of decisions is on sustainable development, at least for the community that the social enterprise is serving. In a sense, the last step in the process is based on business-reflection.

Many organizational leaders take a moment, every five or ten years, to reevaluate their mission and vision to determine if they are still on the right path and if they need to amend their statements to redirect their work. Business-reflection is about the collateral effects of their operations and should be carried out on a yearly basis at a minimum; it suggests that organizational leaders take a moment to perform an introspection of their corporate philosophies and actions toward the co-creation of value. The following questions may be asked to begin the introspection: Why do we do what we do? Is the world a better place because we are in business or are we doing more harm than good? Who and what is affected by our decisions, actions, and results? What are we willing to do to achieve a desired performance? Do the above answers entail ethical and socially responsible practices? Are we holding up our end of our shared responsibilities? Are we socially accountable? Then, importantly, how much harm are we inflicting for the sake of achieving our strategic goals? To be objective, all answers must be backed up by evidence, and properly quantified for their measurement. Then, if needed, corrective action must be taken to ensure that the organization's direct and collateral effects are ethical and socially responsible.

Doing so requires engaging in a decision-making process which involves continuously questioning the long-term effects of all decisions, assessing the current *status quo* and its implications in order to balance the attainment of current goals without compromising future well-being. This decision-making process, illustrated in Fig. 4.4, entails six main steps: (1) establishing a strategic goal (short-term, medium-term, and/or long-term), (2) selecting a set of viable alternatives to achieve the strategic goal, (3) evaluating the alternatives' effects on: strategic goal attainment as well as current generations' well-being, (4) evaluating the alternatives' effects on future organizational outcomes (i.e., the impact on desired performance), as well as consequences for future generations' prosperity, (5) selecting the alternative that both minimizes the negative potential outcomes for the current strategic goal attainment and generations' well-being, and maximizes the positive effect on both future business and social growth and development, and (6) assessing effectivity of the decision over time.

This step in the CASD process serves the purpose of sustainable development which requires a long-term vision and strategic plan to ensure that current practices are enhancing the positive effects in the future. Further, it helps social enterprise leaders continuously evaluate their efforts toward the co-creation of value and added value in each strategic goal in relation to their decision-making. Enterprises can effectively perform an introspection of the organization, actions, results, and

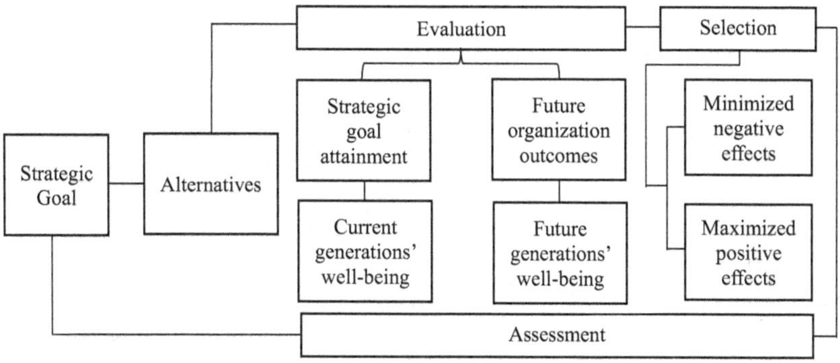

Fig. 4.4 Sustainable development decision-making process

the collateral effects of the latter while creating a system to measure the integration of sustainable development into their decision-making as well as their contribution to sustainable development by means of their actions.

As can be seen, all five steps within the CASD process, as well as the process itself, are cyclical; meaning that, the effectivity and success of co-creating value and added value lays in the ability to make the process habitual or routine. In order to do so, social enterprises could incorporate the process as a corporate practice instilled from top to bottom; for this to be operable, the process should be embedded in the enterprise's corporate philosophy so it may seep through the organization to all strategic goals and into all operations, reaching all internal and external stakeholders, particularly those with whom the enterprise shares responsibility.

The process of co-creating value and added value through sustainable development may help social entrepreneurs increase productivity by means of environmental performance in Latin America and the Caribbean. For instance, a high environmental performance significantly reduces organizational costs which has a positive effect on the organization's business growth; also, such environmental performance positively impacts the quality of the production of natural resources which are used for the enterprise's production of products and/or services (Bovarnick et al., 2010); importantly, the contrary would yield negative results in terms of the persistence of poverty in the region. The process may also assist social enterprise leaders to address poverty education for its reduction and, optimistically, eradication, the enhancement of social health access and quality, and low-cost housing and adequate housing, as catalysts for the sustainable development of Latin America and the Caribbean.

The CASD process, consequently, can have a positive impact on competitiveness at a micro and macro level. That is, as social enterprises share responsibility with other stakeholders on the co-creation of value and added value, they are able to enhance productivity as well as social growth and development of the interested parties which, in turn, will impact the productivity, growth, and development of the country; thus, impacting organizational and country competitiveness. Scaling this process, then, may have a positive effect on global sustainable development; in such a way that the process of co-creating value and added value through sustainable development can help elevate Latin America and the Caribbean from a region with emerging sustainable development, to a developed and sustainable region.

References

Agarwal, S., & Teas, R. T. (2001). Perceived value: Mediating role of perceived risk. *Journal of Marketing Theory and Practice, 9*(4), 1–14. https://doi.org/10.1080/10696679.2001.11501899

Al-Haddad, S., Sharabati, A.-A.A., Al-Khasawneh, M., Maraqa, R., & Hashem, R. (2022). The influence of corporate social responsibility on consumer purchase intention: The mediating role of consumer engagement via social media. *Sustainability, 14*(11), 6771. https://doi.org/10.3390/su14116771

Bianchi, T. (2023). *Social media usage in Latin America—Statistics & Facts*. Statista. Retrieved November 29th, 2023, from: https://www.statista.com/topics/6394/social-media-usage-in-latin-america/#topicOverview

Bice, S., & Jones, K. (2022). Community engagement for urban and regional futures. In R. C. Brears (Ed.), *The Palgrave encyclopedia of urban and regional futures* (pp. 329–340). Palgrave Macmillan.

BID. (2012). *Estudio del BID: América Latina y el Caribe encaran creciente déficit de vivienda*. Retrieved August 14th, 2023 from: https://www.iadb.org/es/noticias/estudio-del-bid-america-latina-y-el-caribe-encaran-creciente-deficit-de-vivienda

Boksberger, P. E., & Melsen, L. (2011). Perceived value: A critical examination of definitions, concepts and measures for the service industry. *Journal of Services Marketing, 25*(3), 229–240. https://doi.org/10.1108/08876041111129209

Boons, F., Montalvo, C., Jaco Quist, J., & Wagner, M. (2013). Sustainable innovation, business models and economic performance: An overview.

Journal of Cleaner Production, 45, 1–8. https://doi.org/10.1016/j.jclepro.2012.08.013

Bovarnick, A., Alpizar, F., & Schnell, C. (2010). *Importance of biodiversity and ecosystems in economic growth and equity in Latin America and the Caribbean: An economic valuation of ecosystems*. Latin America and the Caribbean: A Biodiversity Super Power. New York: UNDP. Retrieved July 10th, 2023, from: https://www.undp.org/sites/g/files/zskgke326/files/publications/Report_ENG.pdf

Boyle, M. E., & Boguslaw, J. (2007). Business, poverty and corporate citizenship. Naming the issues and framing solutions. *Journal of Corporate Citizenship*. 26, 101–120. http://www.jstor.org/stable/jcorpciti.26.101

Boyles, M. (2022). *How do businesses create value for stakeholders?* Harvard Business School Online. Insights. Retrieved August 9th, 2023, from: https://online.hbs.edu/blog/post/how-do-businesses-create-value

Castelán, C. R., Castro, D. S., & Ñopo, H. (2023). *The challenges facing Latin America and the Caribbean in eradicating poverty*. The World Bank. Retrieved November 19th, 2023, from: https://blogs.worldbank.org/latinamerica/challenges-Latin-America-Caribbean-eradicating-poverty

de Chematony, L., Harris, F., & Riley, F. D. (2015). Added value as a source of competitive advantage. In A. Manrai, & H. Meadow, (Eds.) *Global Perspectives in Marketing for the 21st Century. Developments in Marketing Science: Proceedings of the Academy of Marketing Science*. Springer, Cham. https://doi.org/10.1007/978-3-319-17356-6_55

Drucker, P. (1985). *Innovation and entrepreneurship*. Harper & Row.

Dunne, T. C., Aaron, J. R., McDowell, W. C., Urban, D. J., & Geho, P. R. (2016). The impact of leadership on small business innovativeness. *Journal of Business Research, 69*(11), 4876–4881. https://doi.org/10.1016/j.jbusres.2016.04.046

European Parliament. (2023). *Circular economy: definition, importance and benefits*. Economy. Retrieved November 2nd, 2023, from: https://www.europarl.europa.eu/news/en/headlines/economy/20151201STO05603/circular-economy-definition-importance-and-benefits#:~:text=The%20circular%20economy%20is%20a,cycle%20of%20products%20is%20extended.

Filó, C. (2007). *Territorial competitiveness and the human factors*. International Conference of Territorial Intelligence, (pp. 323–336). CAENTI.

Gaiger, L. I., Nyssens, M., & Wanderley, F. (2019). *Social enterprise in Latin America, theory, models and practice*. Routledge.

Hellier, P. K., Geursen, G. M., Carr, R. A., & Rickard, J. A. (2003). Customer repurchase intention: A great structural equation model. *European Journal of Marketing, 37*(11/12), 1762–1800. https://doi.org/10.1108/03090560310495456

Hristov, I., Cimini, R., & Cristofaro, M. (2022). Assessing stakeholders' perception influence on companies' profitability: evidence from Italian companies. *Production planning & control. The management of operations, 35*(3), 308–322. https://doi.org/10.1080/09537287.2022.2078247

Korosec, R. L., & Berman, E. M. (2006). Municipal support for social entrepreneurship. *Public Administration Review, 66*(3), 448–462. https://doi.org/10.1111/j.1540-6210.2006.00601.x

Leadbeater, C. (1997). *The rise of the social entrepreneur*. London: DEMOS. Retrieved April 2nd, 2023, from: https://demos.co.uk/wp-content/uploads/2023/03/theriseofthesocialentrepreneur.pdf

Lederman, D., Messina, J., Pienknagura, S., & Rigolini, J. (2014). *El emprendimiento en América Latina. Muchas empresas y poca innovación*. Banco Internacional de Reconstrucción y Fomento/Banco Mundial. Retrieved April 3rd, 2024, from: https://www.worldbank.org/content/dam/Worldbank/document/LAC/EmprendimientoAmericaLatina_resumen.pdf

Light, P. C. (2009). Social entrepreneurship revisited. *Stanford Social Innovation Review, 7*(3), 21–22. https://doi.org/10.48558/Z8K2-W870

López-Fernández, A. M. (2015). *Convergence of corporate social responsibility and business growth: Collateral effects on business and society*. NOVA Publishers.

López-Fernández, A. M., Terán-Bustamante, A., & Martínez-Velasco, A. (2022). Machine learning sustainable competitiveness for global recovery. In A. M. López-Fernández & A. Terán-Bustamante (Eds.), *Business recovery in emerging markets. Palgrave studies in democracy, innovation, and entrepreneurship for growth* (pp. 241–267). Palgrave Macmillan.

Louati, F. (2018). Knowledge management and the competitiveness of learning organizations. In A. Malheiro, F. Ribeiro, G. L. Jamil, J. P. Rascao, & O. Mealha (Eds.), *Handbook of research on knowledge management for contemporary business environments* (pp. 64–85). IGI Global.

Lukasiewicz, A., Dovers, S., & Eburn, M. (2017). Shared responsibility: The who, what and how. *Environmental Hazards., 16*(4), 291–313. https://doi.org/10.1080/17477891.2017.1298510

Lusch, R. F., & Vargo, S. L. (2006). *The service-dominant logic of marketing: Dialog, debate and directions*. Routledge. https://doi.org/10.4324/9781315699035

OASH. (2023). *Social Determinants of Health*. Office of Disease Prevention and Health Promotion. Priority areas. Retrieved August 8th, 2023, from: https://health.gov/healthypeople/priority-areas/social-determinants-health#:~:text=Social%20determinants%20of%20health%20(SDOH)%20have%20a%20major%20impact%20on,Racism%2C%20discrimination%2C%20and%20violence

Osorio-Novela, G., Mungaray-Lagarda, A., & Ramírez-Angulo, N. (2021). Social enterprise in Mexico, a new business classification. *Sustainability, 13*(16), 9264. https://doi.org/10.3390/su13169264

Ramus, T., & Vaccaro, A. (2017). Stakeholders matter: How Social enterprises address mission drift. *Journal of Business Ethics, 143*, 307–322. https://doi.org/10.1007/s10551-014-2353-y

Roca, H.O. (2005). IV. Hacia la solidaridad en la economía. *Revista Vinculando, 3*(2). Retrieved March 30th, 2024, from: https://vinculando.org/economia_solidaria/humanizar_economia_global/solidaridad_economia_4.html

Shafer, S. M., Smith, H. J., & Linder, J. C. (2005). The power of business models. *Business Horizons, 48*(3), 199–207. https://doi.org/10.1016/j.bushor.2004.10.014

Singh, S., Singh, N., Kalinić, Z., & Liébana-Cabanillas, F. J. (2021). Assessing determinants influencing continued use of live streaming services: An extended perceived value theory of streaming addiction. *Expert Systems with Applications, 168*, 114241. https://doi.org/10.1016/j.eswa.2020.114241

Sinha, I., & Batra, R. (1999). The effect of consumer price consciousness on private label purchase. *International Journal of Research in Marketing, 16*(3), 237–251. https://doi.org/10.1016/S0167-8116(99)00013-0

Solano, S. E., Martínez-Losa, N. A., & Casado, P. P. (2017). Emprendimiento social. *Revista de Estudios de Juventud, 118*, 69–81.

Tuncer, I., Unusan, C., & Cobanoglu, C. (2021). Service quality, perceived value and customer satisfaction on behavioral intention in restaurants: An integrated structural model. *Journal of Quality Assurance in Hospitality and Tourism, 22*(4), 447–475. https://doi.org/10.1080/1528008X.2020.1802390

UN. (2020). *Global Issues. Human Rights*. United Nations. Retrieved October 7th, 2023, from:https://www.un.org/en/global-issues/human-rights#:~:text=International%20human%20rights%20law%20lays,freedoms%20of%20individuals%20or%20groups

UNCTAD. (2023). *Circular Economy*. Retrieved November 2nd, 2023 from: https://unctad.org/es/node/2993

Verbeke, W., Vanhonacker, F., Sioen, I., Van Camp, J., & De Henauw, S. (2007). Perceived importance of sustainability and ethics related to fish: A consumer behavior perspective. *AMBIO: A Journal of the Human Environment., 36*(7), 580–585. https://doi.org/10.1579/0044-7447(2007)36[580:piosae]2.0.co;2

Waddock, S. A., & Post, J. E. (1991). Social entrepreneurs and catalytic change. *Public Administration Review, 51*(5), 393–401. https://doi.org/10.2307/976408

WHO. (2023). *WHO remains firmly committed to the principles set out in the preamble to the Constitution*. Constitution. Retrieved July 18th, 2023, from: https://www.who.int/about/accountability/governance/constitution

Yoo, O. S., & Sarin, R. (2018). Consumer choice and market outcomes under ambiguity in product quality. *Marketing Science, 37*(3), 333–506. https://doi.org/10.1287/mksc.2017.1069

Zauner, A., Koller, M., & Hatak, I. (2015). Customer perceived value—Conceptualization and avenues for future research. *Cogent Psychology, 2*(1), 1061782. https://doi.org/10.1080/23311908.2015.1061782

Zeithaml, V. A. (1988). Consumer perceptions of price, quality, and value: A means-end model and synthesis of evidence. *Journal of Marketing, 52*(3), 2–22. https://doi.org/10.1177/002224298805200302

Zott, C., & Amit, R. (2007). Business model design and the performance of entrepreneurial firms. *Organization Science, 18*(2), 181–199. https://doi.org/10.1287/orsc.1060.0

CHAPTER 5

Social Enterprises: The Road Ahead

Abstract Analyzing certain historic events helps understand the journey to this point; however, assessing the current challenges is essential to learn from the past, take corrective actions, and effectively move toward a future that puts an end to the recurrence of patterns that have been historically limiting. The region's challenges and those for the groups of people in action in social enterprises are key to executing competitive strategies. Further, technology, shared responsibility, and engaging in transformational adoptability for an inclusive, innovative, socially responsible business model that is scalable enables social enterprises to transition from local to global human and sustainable growth and development in the region.

Keywords Regional challenges · Transformational adoptability · Internet of things · Data of things · AI · Collaborative intelligence · Collaborative consumption · Access economy

The history of Latin America and the Caribbean is complex, turbulent, and even violent, from political instability and risk, oppression, to economic crises, environmental exploitation and devastation, social injustice, and insecurity, amongst many other calamities. Now, the reality is

A. M. López-Fernández, *Co-Creation in Social Enterprises*, Palgrave Studies of Entrepreneurship and Social Challenges in Developing Economies, https://doi.org/10.1007/978-3-031-83449-3_5

that this is also true today; there are multiple challenges that countries in Latin America and the Caribbean are still facing in order to achieve sustained development. This chapter puts forth the different challenges that social enterprises will face in the future in Latin America and the Caribbean in order to achieve sustained development and human development, both for the organizations and society. Moreover, the chapter arcs the underlying issue that all organizations should have society's interests in mind while developing their strategic objectives; in other words, the very aspects tackled by social enterprises should be a universal interest.

The region is somewhat of a paradox. It is quite common for people to ponder the question: How can a region so rich in resources be so limited, barely achieve economic growth, or lag so much behind in terms of development? Unless transformational and transcendent change occurs, the question will continue to be posed time and time again. Criticisms of the slow pace toward growth and development in emerging markets are not unfounded. The observed deficiencies have been analyzed and reported by governmental institutions, international organizations, large consulting firms, as well as scholars and researchers; in such a way that there is not only an attempt to shed light on the areas of opportunity, but also to highlight the positive aspects of these markets which, incidentally, draw the attention of potential investors. The fact is that advancements are evidenced by a certain degree of growth; yet, there are underlying aspects that remain unchanged, despite indications of progress, causing great social disparities. The reasons, while multifaceted, are evocative of "*Plus ça change plus c'est la même chose*", meaning, "The more things change, the more they stay the same", an adage credited to Jean-Baptiste Alphonse Karr in *1849*. In a sense, despite the region's progress, there are a series of variables, policies, and standards that continue to enable the slow or lack of growth and human and sustainable development.

We are living in a time when the most constant variable is change. Does it not seem as though this statement has been fitting for just about every decade and every year? Just in the last three years, the region has experienced catastrophic natural disasters, the deployment of armies, severe inflation, extemporaneous elections, strikes, protests, etc.; that is, a series of events that have continuously jeopardized the region's democracy. Furthermore, Latin America and the Caribbean was hit the hardest by the COVID-19 pandemic (The World Bank, 2023b) causing important setbacks in relation to economic growth and social development. Therefore, if the last years have taught us anything, it is that life altering events occur in a blink of an eye, and being prepared, as much as possible, is a must to be able to face challenges head-on.

It is fair to say that the region is reasonably resilient given the multifaceted challenges it has faced. Resilience has become a common word for a variety of situations, such as competition, surviving trauma or a crisis, tolerating unethical behavior, overcoming obstacles and challenges, etc. A good example is how, despite the current economic downfalls of some countries, there is an important indicator of economic growth; Latin America's gross domestic product grew about 2 percent in 2023 which, although somewhat higher than in 2022, was lower than the growth in other regions (The World Bank, 2023a). What is more, the economic growth some countries display seems to be against all odds as human development indicators are still lagging. There are far too many people struggling to break the poverty cycle, thus, an additional layer of the region's paradox.

In addition, it is also a region that is highly attractive for investors. In fact, according to a KPMG study with four hundred business leaders, investors see Latin America and the Caribbean as an important region as 45 percent of companies and investors agree that it is an opportunity for mergers and acquisitions (M&G) while still recognizing that there are associated risks (35 percent) (KPMG, 2023) with such investments; therefore, there is a perception of high risks and high rewards. This means that there is indication of potential micro and macro growth in the region. Furthermore, the United Nations work group on business and human rights, in relation to the project on Responsible business conduct in Latin America and the Caribbean (CERALC), has developed a report which highlights the importance of including human rights in financial activity. Despite the fact that financial institutions and investors have been pursuing more social and environmental concerns in their decision-making, the incessant violations of human rights as well as the environment's exploitation and destruction, are clear indicators that sustainable finance is insufficient (CERALC, 2023) for a significant, transformative, and much needed change.

General Challenges in the Region

The general challenges that persist in Latin America and the Caribbean act as a type of baseline for the challenges that people in action in social enterprises currently face and are most likely to face in the future. Said challenges include a historic legacy, the current state of affairs related to poverty, social health, and housing, opportunities for micro, small, and medium-sized enterprises, and cultural dimensions; these will be briefly discussed in this section.

A Historic Legacy

Since the fifteenth century, Latin America and the Caribbean has been viewed as "discoverable" land, a paradise, and excellent opportunity for investment and growth. History repeats itself; it informs much of the current realities that societies face, the good, the bad, and the atrocious. Historic repetitiveness, or recurrence, is indicative of the fact that when lessons are not fully understood those in action are destined to repeat the same behaviors and attain the same or very similar results. Destined not because it is already in the cards, but because the attitudes and behavior do not display sufficient change for results to be significantly different.

Although the region is much more democratic, the turbulent history of conquests, colonialism, and dictatorships has definitely impacted social growth and development. The aftermath of colonialism and dictatorships is unsurprisingly still thriving. However different the methods and the individuals assuming positions of power, the patterns of control in Latin America and the Caribbean persist much like during colonial times (Castro-Lara, 2016). Some countries in the region are in continuous conflict with political and economic instability which does nothing to change the negative impact on the populations' lack of trust and credibility in their institutions; it not only exacerbates a hierarchical system, classism, and resentment, but also negatively impacts consumption as well as the countries' gross domestic product (Zevallos, 2003). Therefore, the instability of Latin American and Caribbean countries has not only led to complex social systems that cause intermittent growth and staggering development but is also responsible for seven main current challenges:

1. Articulating public policy to enable long-term planning, beyond governments' current terms, for social growth and development.
2. Shifting leadership's mindset; that is, it is imperative to change the lingering colonizer frame of mind as this is the only way the region will progress toward democratization.
3. Adopting transformational policies for scalability.
4. Renovating public institutions as well as obsolete infrastructure.

5. Diversifying production and economies.
6. Transparently addressing corruption and impunity.
7. Building trust and credibility.

The Current State of Affairs

In the first chapter, the current status of the region, in relation to the HDI and SDGs, on poverty, housing, and health was discussed. Housing is problematic in societies in Latin America and the Caribbean, particularly for the most vulnerable; about 23 million individuals in the region experience housing shortage, and about 46 million experience deficiencies in housing quality (López, 2023). In addition, just like in other regions, the younger generations, Generations Y and Z, are finding it difficult to purchase housing; the constant increase in prices and disproportionate increase in salaries has decreased the possibility for younger generations to purchase a house. Access to adequate health attention is still problematic in the region and is directly correlated with persistent inequalities. Latin America and the Caribbean continues to survive a health crisis, exacerbated by the COVID-19 Pandemic (PAHO, 2023), as well as the fact that over 22 percent lack sufficient resources to access and maintain a healthy diet (OPS, 2023).

Poverty does not only refer to the gap between the haves and the have-nots in relation to financial income and stability, rather it is also considered to be observed when individuals lack specific and basic needs related to food, health, housing, safety, and security (Bradshaw, 2009). Therefore, tackling poverty in Latin America and the Caribbean should be a primary concern of social enterprises in the hopes to address housing and health issues as well. Put simply, social development goals related to housing and health cannot be attained if goals related to extreme poverty and poverty are not effectively achieved and managed.

In addition, particular challenges include closing the gender gap; that is, in terms of equal access to opportunities, education, technology, healthcare, representation, and equal and fair compensation, amongst others. The gender gap is not only unacceptable but also creates one of the greatest impediments to sustainable development. About 50.8 percent of the population in Latin America and the Caribbean are women (The World Bank, 2023c) and they are disproportionately neglected. This means that over half of the population, which is at higher risk for falling into poverty, has fewer means to accelerate sustainable development as they do not have the same opportunities as men, and a significant proportion of them are leading micro, small, and medium enterprises, and social enterprises. As the gender gap exacerbates poverty, ignoring the former reduces the probability of eradicating the latter. The importance lies in the fact that poverty brings other development variables to a halt; people living in poverty and extreme poverty are unable to access basic services, and satisfy their basic needs, which means that there is significant difficulty to access education, social health, and housing which, in turn, exacerbates the cycle of poverty.

In other words, regulatory authorities have an important responsibility to eradicate poverty and extreme poverty; in fact, some might argue that it is solely their responsibility, however, it has become clear that it is or ought to be a shared responsibility. Suppose that regulatory authorities worked toward the eradication of poverty and extreme poverty, if at a micro level organizations did not do their part toward the same end (i.e., did not eliminate practices of labor exploitation and unfair compensation), poverty would persist; thus, perpetuating the cycle of poverty, inaccessibility to health services, and insufficient housing. Further, facing challenges related to access as well as to quality, and addressing them may help in the reduction of disparities in the region, as well as strengthen the agencies in charge of ensuring that human rights are not violated.

mSMEs

Another challenge has to do with the number of organizations that are in the informal economy. In emerging markets and developing countries, micro enterprises make up the majority of organizations, particularly in the informal economy (Vandenberg, 2009). Micro and small enterprises, which have the ability to influence social growth and development, require strong incentives backed by public policy to transition to the formal economy. Of course, doing so is not an easy task, this is evidenced by the policies that are currently in place in countries in the region that have not yielded the desired results. Reasons include persistent corruption, impunity, misinformation, and lack of business, financial, and fiscal education; in a sense, for many entrepreneurs the idea of transitioning into the formal economy seems baffling and nonsensical. The fact of the matter is that the informal economy negatively impacts sustainable development, even more so within emerging markets and developing countries. Businesses operating in the informal sector certainly have a negative impact on the country's economy, however, there are also negative implications for human development as, for instance, workers are not protected and tend to be unfairly compensated, which affects their quality of life and that of their families.

Small and medium-sized enterprises are extremely important because they mobilize the economy and create jobs, even though it might not be done in the desired manner, and they have a significant ability to innovate, all of which are essential to social enterprises' operations. Despite efforts to create infrastructure to promote small and medium enterprises, they continue to face certain challenges particularly in Latin America and the Caribbean; for instance, they continue to experience "lack of access to financing, bureaucracy, informality, unfair competition and difficulties in accessing international markets" (Sforza, 2023). Meaning that, even those that are part of the formal sector are continuously struggling between survival and growth.

Cultural Dimensions

Culture is as relevant as the structures and systems created and imposed in and for societies' growth and development. Cultural dimensions, such as individualism and collectivism, and power distance (The Culture Factor, 2023) are particularly relevant on the road toward social change. Societies in Latin America and the Caribbean have been widely acknowledged as sharing a collectivist behavior in terms of their shared values; however, in contrast to common belief, they are also independent (Krys et al., 2022) in terms of the way in which they perceive themselves in relation to others, that is, the construals of themselves or self-construals (Markus & Kitayama, 1991). Further, a study carried out with senior managers shows that the region places immense importance on family collectivism and group loyalty, and although its societies exhibit individualistic traits, there is a strong commitment toward the precedence of common good over personal gains (Ogliastri et al., 1999). Naturally, individualism has increased over the decades thanks to globalization, the ubiquitousness of the Internet and social media, and as a means for self-preservation. Most countries in Latin America and the Caribbean also display a high-power distance; societies are not only unequal but also have a certain degree of acceptance of power being distributed unequally, which is most likely a behavior inherited from generation to generation as an effect of colonialism, as well as perceived hierarchy of credibility (Becker, 1967). The cultural aspect points to two other particular challenges:

1. Recognizing that shared history and traits also require a shared understanding of the current state of affairs, of oppression, to work toward social change.
2. Increasing awareness of the need for shared responsibility adopted on the basis of shared values.

The fact that countries in Latin America and the Caribbean are still lagging in terms of social development is a clear indication that there is a need for additional assistance; for such reasons, social enterprises have become increasingly important and key to driving progress. Therefore, given their degree of importance, it is essential to create strategies that enable these organizations to work effectively in the market and, thus, yield necessary results for sustainable development. As mentioned in previous chapters, social enterprises are not exempt from the business aspects of any organization; particularly, these organizations require a successful business model, effective stakeholder management, strategic decision-making, which requires timely information and data, flexibility for innovation and creativity, as well as capital and resources.

It has become clear that: (i) much work is needed in order to successfully reach the desired state of social development, (ii) governments and regulatory authorities cannot fix the social problem without external assistance, and (iii) social enterprises have the ability to influence social change and aid in the attainment of human and sustainable development. Which brings us to the challenges of social enterprises, more specifically, the challenges of the people in action in social enterprises.

Challenges for People in Action

The first group of people in action, described in Chapter 1, are those that historically took part in shaping the current state of affairs (i.e., politically, economically, socially, and culturally) of the countries in Latin America and the Caribbean. They are no longer current people in action as they are not in power or with us; however, this does not mean that there is no longer a first group in action. Current regulatory authorities now take on the role of the first group of people in action in social enterprises because their decisions and actions still shape the current *status quo* of social well-being in the region. Further, they are a stakeholder in social enterprises and, therefore, also part of the third group of people in action whose participation is elemental to social enterprises' effective operations. Moreover, the performance of social enterprises and regulatory authorities are mutually benefited by their collaboration and shared responsibility. As such, their actions could include:

1. Developing public policy that enables social enterprises to tackle extreme poverty and poverty as well as housing and social health issues in parallel to their efforts.
2. Strengthening existing agencies and institutions to ensure that human rights are upheld.
3. Creating systems that instill accountability in relation to goal achievement associated with poverty, health, and housing.
4. Partnering with social enterprises to pool needed resources, capital, and infrastructure to tackle poverty, health, and housing issues.
5. Founding and funding state-driven social enterprise programs focused on poverty, health, and housing.

The second group of people in action in social enterprises, discussed in Chapter 2, are the architects, leaders of social enterprises, also known as sociopreneurs. They face challenges related to insufficient resources and infrastructure, and lack of innovation and cooperation to achieve their objectives, increase their scope of action, and scale the organization. As such, their actions could include:

1. Designing a corporate philosophy descriptive of the level of responsibility, accountability, and inclusiveness with which the enterprise will operate.
2. Adopting a democratic, transformational, and/or socially responsible leadership style fit for an inclusive and innovative business model.
3. Acquiring funding for necessary resources and infrastructure.
4. Partnering with private and public sector organizations.
5. Developing an inclusive and sustained business model.
6. Managing their stakeholder network effectively.

7. Co-creating added value through sustainable development.
8. Scaling up the organization to achieve the social mission—locally and globally.

The third group of people in action in social enterprises is their interested parties, that is, their stakeholders. As described in the previous chapter, a successful social enterprise co-creates value with the active and proactive participation of the organization's stakeholders. Therefore, their actions could include:

1. Expanding partnerships with private and public organizations (for-profit and not-for-profit) locally, nationally, and/or globally, starting within their corresponding supply chains.
2. Participating in the creation of innovative and creative solutions for the reduction of poverty and extreme poverty, enhancement of social health, and housing.
3. Engaging with social enterprises to achieve their social mission.
4. Shifting—Exhibiting a high use of their voice regarding social issues as well as high levels of action
5. Taking collective action to alleviate social injustice, social inequality, as well as environmental devastation
6. Co-creating value and added value through shared responsibility for social change

The fourth group of people in action in social enterprises is those that receive the benefits, or the value, of the results of the enterprise's operations. These are not the consumers of the products and/or services offered by organizations, rather, they are the beneficiaries who are positively impacted by the social enterprise's social mission, their purpose. In order to take action in social enterprises, they need to consider accessibility and affordability of available products and/or services that social enterprises may offer to assist in the social issue that negatively affects them, as well as willingness to associate with the social enterprise in question to participate in the co-creation of value and added value for all interested parties.

Organizations can no longer afford to solely focus on their success, whether it be their bottom line, market share, volume of business, competitiveness, or perpetuity. There are a variety of aspects that permeate society and threaten human development and, therefore, have both direct and indirect effects on organizations' survivability and, thus, successful performance. To expand the notion of success and create the foundation for social enterprises to face current and future challenges, it is suggested that they engage in transformational adoptability.

Organizations and individuals in Latin America and the Caribbean are highly resilient. This is not only observed in their turbulent history, but also with more current major disruptors such as the health pandemic which, as previously mentioned, had a particularly negative impact on the region. One of the consequences has been that the youngest generations have had a crash course in trauma, crisis management, work dynamics, and financial strains, amongst others. This certainly influences their behavior in terms of education, work, and consumption in general.

The main problem does not seem to reside in their resilience, rather in transformational adoptability. It is a prominent challenge for organizations in Latin America and the Caribbean. The fact of the matter is that organizations, and society in general, in the region have an impressive ability to adapt to adverse circumstances; there is a somewhat unhealthy level of acceptance that comes far too quickly when faced with instability, risk, crisis, and overall unfavorable events. However, as opposed to adaptability, adoptability entails the ability to successfully accept and execute a new system, method, and/or process. In order to take advantage of transformative opportunities, such as new technologies and innovations, it is indispensable that individuals and organizations address underlying issues such as resistance to change, lack of resources, training and development, and the tendency toward indulgence and complacency, amongst other limitations. It is even more difficult to adopt a transformative mindset, however necessary to enact social change. Though people's resilience is elemental when facing these challenges, it is not enough for the radical change needed to ensure human and sustainable growth and development in the region.

In order to engage in transformational adoptability, social entrepreneurs should consider the cultural dimensions as key factors for transformation as well as change in general; and bearing in mind that the creation of the enterprise can potentially provide labor opportunities, their purpose may prompt innovative solutions (Setiawan et al., 2023), and value and added value may be co-created for all interested parties, particularly, for those experiencing the negative effects of social injustice and inequality. Then, sociopreneurs may design, develop, and execute strategies related to: problem-setting, innovativeness, collective intelligence, the Internet of Things (IoT), collaborative intelligence, collaborative consumption, access economy, partnerships, and SDG alignment, which are discussed below.

Social enterprises may benefit from enhanced stakeholder participation by engaging in problem-setting (Diefenthaler, 2008) and problem-solving. In order to do so, sociopreneurs can:

1. Identify a social and/or environmental issue that they wish to address with the enterprise's social mission.
2. Analyze the issue to determine the root cause.
3. Research the market, particularly: beneficiaries of the social mission and target audience (consumers of products and/or services to be offered).
4. Design alternative solutions for the social and/or environmental issue.
5. Develop a corporate philosophy that enables the achievement of profit with purpose.
6. Select the alternative that best solves the social and/or environmental issue.
7. Manage their current stakeholder network for goal achievement.
8. Execute the selected solution.
9. Evaluate the results and performance of the selected solution.
10. Implement corrective actions, where applicable.

Innovation is and will be required to achieve sustainable development and, therefore, for the fulfillment of the 2030 Agenda (UNECE, 2023). Thus, it makes sense that social enterprises develop strategies that enhance organizational innovativeness to assist in the design and creation of inclusive solutions. The intent is to focus on cutting-edge innovations, which may or may not be disruptive, but are certainly socially responsible and sustainable.

Collective intelligence, which is derived from the synergy generated by the sum of individuals' efforts exerted while performing their tasks (Floresa et al., 2015), is positively impacted by the Internet and social media (Gregg, 2010). Globalization and the Internet of Things have made it possible for jobs, products, services, content, art, ideas, etc., to be global; in other words, individuals and organizations have the opportunity to globally leave a mark, even miles away from their residence. There is an opportunity, given the current state of hyperconnectivity to co-create value via the Internet, people, and data of things (Ziouvelou & McGroarty, 2021); thus, social enterprises may foster collective intelligence locally and globally by making use of the Internet of Things to create innovative solutions to social issues.

Collaborative intelligence occurs when the strengths of collaborators are worked in conjunction with Artificial Intelligence (AI) in order to enhance performance (Wilson & Daugherty, 2018). In other words, it entails working with AI instead of merely automating process and procedures to replace collaborators with AI. Although great ideas may start small, in order to have a greater impact social enterprises must delegate efforts toward scaling up (Light, 2009). Developing a collaborative intelligence strategy is particularly beneficial for social enterprises that have entered the scalability stage of growth.

Collaborative consumption is a direct response to the social, environmental, and financial concerns of entrepreneurs as well as consumers (Tussyadiah, 2015). It occurs as individuals share resources, which is why it is also known as peer-to-peer exchange (Perren & Grauerholz, 2015). The structure includes organizations that operate as intermediaries, now more commonly found on online platforms, between individuals providing and acquiring services (Perren & Grauerholz, 2015). Social enterprises may design collaborative consumption strategies when their core business is best offered online as intermediaries, or in the early stages of growth when resources and infrastructure tend to be virtually nonexistent.

With access economy organizations are able to profit from resources that are not used to their full potential; that is, consumers "from individuals to business entities, from micro to large businesses coming from developed and developing countries, can share unutilized resources, products, and/or services by means of a third-party provider, typically an app or digital platform" (Omazić et al., 2023, pg. 15); in such a way that social enterprises may make use of access economy to reduce costs related to resources that they can otherwise not afford to purchase but that could positively impact their operations and, therefore, goal achievement. Furthermore, sociopreneurs may receive additional income from any underutilized resources they own and decide to temporarily rent.

Partnerships that bring various stakeholders together are a particular area of opportunity in Latin America and the Caribbean (Peregalli & Ochoa, 2023); however, social enterprises may partner with both private and public sector organizations. According to a study developed by Deloitte, organizational leaders are taking a stronger stance and interest in social performance; their results indicate that 84 percent consider well-being to be important, and 77 percent stated that citizenship and social impact are also important, however, only 49 percent and 51 percent, respectively, state to be prepared to meet the expectations (Deloitte, 2018). In other words, while they consider these aspects important, they are not prepared to generate substantial results for sustainable development. Partnering with these organizations could potentially bring together all groups of people in action in social enterprises, therefore, increasing the probability of a successful performance and, in turn, of sustainable development.

Every country, even within the same region, has its own particular legislative system as well as internal policies that address, or attempt to address, social well-being and welfare. The region of Latin America and the Caribbean is no exception. For such matter, it is necessary to take international guidelines into consideration in order to be able to effectively assess the current state of social development, or lack thereof. As mentioned in previous chapters, a suitable set of guidelines may be drawn from the United Nations sustainable development goals and the 2030 Agenda (UNDG, 2018). It is important to remember that the 2030 Agenda works toward sustainable development, which entails doing for the present generation without compromising the needs of future generations; in such a way that social enterprises' decisions which are made today should include practices that will not compromise current sustainable development and will enhance the sustainable development of future generations.

According to the Global Entrepreneurship Monitor report, about half of entrepreneurship in 75 percent of the studied countries consider the sustainable development goals a priority (GEM, 2023). This indicates that there is potential to align strategic organizational goals with the sustainable development goals. What is more, the probability of social enterprises succeeding increases with the existence of sustainable development (Setiawan et al., 2023). Furthermore, developing strategies related to partnerships and SDG alignment means that social enterprises may work alongside other types of organizations and governments (i.e., share responsibility) toward the achievement of national, regional, and global sustainable development.

From Local to Global Co-Created Added Value

The global panorama is observed as a state of polycrisis which has a direct and negative impact on sustainable development (Bonnici et al., 2024). It is time to move forward, and beyond the notion that productivity, financial performance, and economic prosperity should be the highest priority of State leaders, as well as organizational leaders across the board of industries, sectors, and regions. Co-creating value and added value in social enterprises can be done because of all four groups of people taking action, as well as for them. Elevating the impacts of social enterprises' social mission to a global sphere is possible by designing strategies fit for scalability. Figure 5.1 includes the effects of scalable social enterprises. That is, engaging in transformational adoptability for an inclusive, innovative, socially responsible business model that is scalable. In other words, the same actions and strategies described above in the chapter may be redesigned to achieve goals locally as well as globally.

Social enterprises in Latin America and the Caribbean should take advantage of the ubiquitousness of, for instance, social media and social networking sites, to scale their operations locally, nationally, and internationally. More often than not, the four groups of people in action are local, however, social enterprises have the potential to expand their influence and impact regionally and globally. In fact, the issues tackled

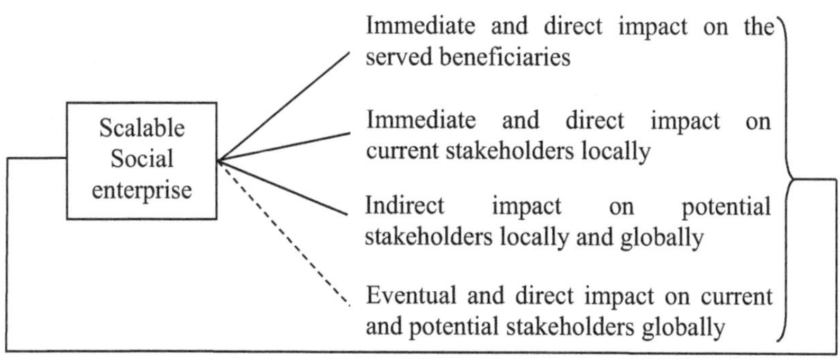

Fig. 5.1 Effects of scalable social enterprises

by social entrepreneurs include social and environmental matters which, although may begin with small initiatives, certainly have global implications (Santos, 2012); a clear example is the fact that social enterprises can help accelerate the eradication of poverty (Setiawan et al., 2023). It is true that social and environmental issues have a ripple effect, which means that they have direct negative impacts as well as a potentially large reach of indirect negative effects; that being said, both effects apply positively for social and environmental solutions that are inclusive, innovative, and socially responsible.

Profit with Purpose Beyond Social Enterprises

If we look back and analyze the evolution of management, we can see that, in some instances, little has changed since the onset of classical administration. There are still organizations whose predominant focus is efficiency and productivity, with income and profit as the primary objectives. However, the increasingly turbulent times require effective, resilient, responsive, and responsible management, or a holistic approach to management is required. With all the lessons learned throughout history and given recent events, it should be unsurprising that solely focusing on the bottom line is no longer sufficient to (*i*) sustain in the market successfully, or (*ii*) address the negative effects of delaying the achievement of sustainable development.

The burden of social development cannot fall solely on the region's governments or social enterprises for that matter. The very social and environmental issues that social enterprises tackle should, at the very least, be a concern of all organizations. Regardless of organizations' size and core business, or the industries and sectors they operate in, they have a certain degree of stake in society. In that they are dependent on society's actions to sustain in the market; thus, it is also in their interest to pursue profit with a purpose. In order to do so, all organizations need to delegate significant efforts toward a proactive participation in human development and sustainable development.

As previously mentioned, poverty, social health, and housing are interrelated and directly impact sustainable development. Health, for instance, is elemental to achieve inclusive social development, sustainability, and economic growth (Marinho et al., 2023); and, as poverty is a strong determinant of social health and housing, it makes sense to challenge all organizational leaders to question the effect of their decisions and actions in relation to theses aspects and take corrective actions. There are organizations that have made a significant effort to operate in an ethical, sustainable, and socially responsible manner. For instance, according to Cezarino et al., (2022), in emerging markets, such as those in Latin America and the Caribbean, social development is often instigated by organizations' engagement in corporate social responsibility as well as social enterprises. However, the road toward achieving sustainable development is still slow. Meaning, a business model that enables transformational adoptability by attaining profit with purpose is a challenge for all organizations, not just social enterprises. The questions, then, must be: are organizations in the region ready and willing to redesign and align their corporate philosophy, governance, and culture, to a strategic socially responsible approach to sustainable development? Are they ready to prioritize the adoption of sustainable development goals as strategic organizational goals? And are they ready to take on the eradication of poverty, the fortification of social health, and improvement of housing? Only then will our collective decisions and actions co-create added value and genuinely benefit current and potential stakeholders and current and future generations.

References

Becker, H. S. (1967). Whose side are we on? *Social Problems, 14*(3), 239–247. https://doi.org/10.2307/799147

Bonnici, F., Klijn, V., Nowack, D., Bennett, T., & Gregory, D. (2024). *The State of Social Enterprise: A Review of Global Data 2013–2023. Insight Report*. SCHWAB Foundation & The World Economic Forum. Retrieved May 8th, 2024, from: https://www3.weforum.org/docs/WEF_The_State_of_Social_Enterprise_2024.pdf

Bradshaw, T. K. (2009). Theories of poverty and anti-poverty programs in community development. *Community Development, 38*(1), 7–25. https://doi.org/10.1080/15575330709490182

Castro-Lara, E. (2016). Reflexiones para decolonizar la cultura académica latinoamericana en Comunicación. *Chasqui. Revista Latinoamericana de Comunicación, 131*, 107–122.

CERALC. (2023). *Se lanza informe sobre finanzas y DDHH en América Latina y el Caribe*. Actividades. Retrieved December 24th, 2023, from: https://empresasyderechoshumanos.org/actividad/se-lanza-informe-sobre-finanzas-y-ddhh-en-america-latina-y-el-caribe/#:~:text=En%20esta%20nota%20informativa%20el%20Grupo%20de%20Trabajo,operan%20all%C3%AD%2C%20tanto%20bancos%20comerciales%20como%20inversionistas%20institucionales%2C

Cezarino, L. O., Liboni, L. B., Hunter, T., Pacheco, L. M., & Martins, F. P. (2022). Corporate social responsibility in emerging markets: Opportunities and challenges for sustainability integration. *Journal of Cleaner Production, 362*, 132224. https://doi.org/10.1016/j.jclepro.2022.132224

Diefenthaler, A. (2008). Problem setting. In M. Erlhoff, & T. Marshall, (Eds). *Design dictionary. Board of International Research in Design*. Birkhäuser Basel. https://doi.org/10.1007/978-3-7643-8140-0_208

Deloitte. (2018). *The rise of the social enterprise 2018 Deloitte Global Human Capital Trends*. Retrieved September 9th, 2023, from: https://www2.deloitte.com/content/dam/insights/us/articles/HCTrends2018/2018-HCtrends_Rise-of-the-social-enterprise.pdf

Floresa, R. L., Negny, S., Belaud, J. P., & Lann, J.-M.L. (2015). Collective intelligence to solve creative problems in conceptual design phase. *Procedia Engineering, 13*, 850–860. https://doi.org/10.1016/j.proeng.2015.12.394

GEM. (2023). *Global Entrepreneurship Monitor 2023/2024 Global Report: 25 Years and Growing*. GEM.

Gregg, D. G. (2010). Designing for collective intelligence. *Communications of the ACM, 53*(4), 134–138. https://doi.org/10.1145/1721654.1721691

KPMG. (2023). *In an uncertain world, LATAM M&A is on the rise. KPGM 2023 M&A in Latam survey*. Retrieved October 22nd, 2023, from: https://assets.kpmg.com/content/dam/kpmg/xx/pdf/2023/06/m-a-in-latin-america-english-report.pdf

Krys, K., Vignoles, V. L., de Almeida, I., & Uchida, Y. (2022). Outside the "Cultural Binary": Understanding why Latin American collectivist societies foster independent selves. *Perspectives on Psychological Science, 17*(4), 1166–1187. https://doi.org/10.1177/17456916211029632

Light, P. C. (2009). Social entrepreneurship revisited. *Stanford Social Innovation Review, 7*(3), 21–22. https://doi.org/10.48558/Z8K2-W870

López, P. (2023). *Vivienda asequible en América Latina y el Caribe*. Banco de Desarrollo de América Latina y el Caribe (CAF). Retrieved May 2nd, 2024, from: https://www.caf.com/es/conocimiento/visiones/2023/08/vivienda-asequible-en-america-latina-y-el-caribe/

Marinho, M. L., Dahuabe, A., & de Mesa, A. A. (2023). *Salud y desigualdad en América Latina y el Caribe. La centralidad de la salud para el desarrollo social inclusivo y sostenible*. Serie Políticas Sociales No 244 (LC/TS.2023/115), Comisión Económica para América Latina y el Caribe (CEPAL). Retrieved

May 13th, 2024, from: https://repositorio.cepal.org/server/api/core/bitstreams/b816a7eb-10d7-4f37-8eba-e6cb8feb91cc/content

Markus, H. R., & Kitayama, S. (1991). Culture and the self: Implications for cognition, emotion, and motivation. *Psychological Review.*, *98*(2), 224–253. https://doi.org/10.1037/0033-295X.98.2.224

Omazić, M. A., Labaš, D., & Uroić, P. (2023). Access economy (ethics). In S. O. Idowu, R. Schmidpeter, N. Capaldi, L. Zu, M. Del Baldo, & R. Abreu (Eds.), *Encyclopedia of sustainable management* (pp. 15–22). Springer.

Ogliastri, E., McMillen, C., Altschul, C., Arias, M. E., de Bustamante, C., Dávila, C., Dorfman, P., dela Coletta, M. F., Fimmen, C., Ickis, J., & Martínez, S. (1999). Cultura y liderazgo organizacional en 10 países de América Latina. El estudio Globe Academia. *Revista Latinoamericana de Administración*, *22*, 29–57. https://www.proquest.com/scholarly-journals/cultura-y-liderazgo-organizacional-en-10-países/docview/912166953/se-2

OPS. (2023). *Informe ONU: 131 millones de personas en América Latina y el Caribe no pueden acceder a una dieta saludable*. Organización Panamericana de la Salud. Retrieved May 14th, 2023, from: https://www.paho.org/es/noticias/19-1-2023-informe-onu-131-millones-personas-america-latina-caribe-no-pueden-acceder-dieta#:~:text=En%20el%20Caribe%2C%20un%2052,una%20dieta%20saludable%20en%202020.

PAHO. (2023). *Salud en las Américas 2022. Panorama de la Región de las Américas en el contexto de la pandemia de COVID-19*. Pan American Health Organization. Publicaciones Generales. Retrieved September 21st, 2023, from: https://iris.paho.org/handle/10665.2/56471

Peregalli, A., & Ochoa, E. (2023). Higher education and social engagement in Latin America. In R. Munck, Y. Pinilla, R. A. Hodges, & C. Bartch (Eds.), *Higher Education in Latin America and the Caribbean Civic engagement and the democratic mission* (pp. 60–77). Machdohnil Ltd.

Perren, R., & Grauerholz, L. (2015). Collaborative consumption. *International Encyclopedia of the Social & Behavioral Sciences, 4*, 139–144. https://doi.org/10.1016/B978-0-08-097086-8.64143-0

Santos, F. M. (2012). A positive theory of social entrepreneurship. *Journal of Business Ethics, 111*(3), 335–351. https://doi.org/10.1007/s10551-012-1413-4

Setiawan, H. H., Yuda, T. K., Susantyo, B., Sulubere, M. B., Ganti, M., Habibullah, H., Sabarisman, M., & Murni, R. (2023). Scaling up social entrepreneurship to reduce poverty: Exploring the challenges and opportunities through stakeholder engagement. *Frontiers in Sociology.*, *8*, 1131762. https://doi.org/10.3389/fsoc.2023.1131762

Sforza, O. R. (2023). *Latinoamerica y el Caribe: Las pymes son fundamentales para el crecimiento de la región*. Cátedra Avícola Latam. Retrieved

November 27th, 2023, from: https://catedralatam.com/latinoamerica-y-el-caribe-las-pymes-son-fundamentales-para-el-crecimiento-de-la-region/

The Culture Factor. (2023). *Country Comparison Tool*. Retrieved November 11th, 2023, from: https://www.hofstede-insights.com/country-comparison-tool

The World Bank. (2023a). Economic Review. Latin America and the Caribbean October 2023. Report Sections. Retrieved November 16th, 2023, from: https://www.worldbank.org/en/region/lac/publication/perspectivas-economicas-america-latina-caribe#:~:text=The%20report%20estimates%20that%20the,for%202024%20and%202025%2C%20respectively.

The World Bank. (2023b). *COVID-19 (Coronavirus) Response*. The World Bank in Latin America and the Caribbean. Retrieved November 4th, 2023, from: https://www.worldbank.org/en/region/lac/coronavirus

The World Bank. (2023c). Population, female (% of total population)—Latin America & Caribbean. Latin America & Caribbean Data. Retrieved May 4th, 2024, from: https://data.worldbank.org/indicator/SP.POP.TOTL.FE.ZS?locations=ZJ

Tussyadiah, I. (2015). An exploratory on drivers and deterrents of collaborative consumption in travel. In I. Tussyadiah & A. Inversini (Eds.), *Information & communication technologies in tourism 2015*. Springer International Publishing.

UNDG. (2018). *Challenges and strategies for sustainable development in Latin America and the Caribbean*. Sustainable Development Group of the United Nations. Retrieved April 18th, 2023, from: https://unsdg.un.org/sites/default/files/Challenges-and-Strategies-for-Sustainable-Development-in-Latin-America-and-the-Caribbean.pdf

UNECE. (2023). *Innovation and Competitiveness Policies (ICP). Introduction*. United Nations Economic Commission for Europe. Retrieved December 19th, 2023, from: https://unece.org/economic-cooperation-and-integration/innovation-and-competitiveness-policies-icp

Vandenberg, P. (2009). *Micro, Small and Medium-Sized Enterprises and the Global Economic Crisis. Impacts and Policy Responses*. International Labour Organization (ILO). Retrieved November 10th, 2023, from: https://www.ilo.org/wcmsp5/groups/public/---ed_emp/---emp_ent/documents/publication/wcms_108413.pdf

Wilson, H. J., & Daugherty, P. R. (2018). Collaborative Intelligence: Humans and AI are joining forces. Humans and machines can enhance each other's strengths. *Harvard Business Review*. 114–123. Retrieved August 11th, 2023, from: https://hbr.org/2018/07/collaborative-intelligence-humans-and-ai-are-joining-forces

Zevallos, E.V. (2003). Micro, pequeñas y medianas empresas en América Latina. *Revista de la CEPAL*. *79*, 53–70. Retrieved November 18th,

2023 from: https://repositorio.cepal.org/server/api/core/bitstreams/73fcf4cf-9b77-44c1-94ab-d810f65be455/content

Ziouvelou, X., & McGroarty, F. (2021). *Emerging ecosystem-centric business models for sustainable value creation*. IGI Global.

Index

A. M. López-Fernández, *Co-Creation in Social Enterprises*, Palgrave Studies of Entrepreneurship and Social Challenges in Developing Economies, https://doi.org/10.1007/978-3-031-83449-3

FSC
www.fsc.org
MIX
Papier | Fördert gute Waldnutzung
FSC® C083411

Kolibri 360 GmbH
Ferdinand-Jühlke-Straße 7
99095 Erfurt, Deutschland
produktsicherheit@kolibri360.de